Praise for

PLAN B

"No matter what you're going through, *Plan B* will help you get through it. *Plan B* is a down-to-earth book written by a down-to-earth pastor. Authentic hope is only a book away!"

> — **Mark Batterson**
> senior pastor, National
> Community Church,
> and author of *Primal*

"Pete Wilson is a young, dynamic leader with a growing church and a heart to see people reach out and find Christ in the midst of any and every circumstance. His sincerity and desire to disarm some of life's difficult twists and turns with godly perspective will help anyone struggling with life's realities and Plan B."

> — **Brian Houston**
> senior pastor, Hillsong Church

"Hope is packaged and sold in many different ways in our society, often wrapped with false promises and an unrealistic view of life. This is why *Plan B* is such an important book. Pete deals openly and honestly with the disappointments we experience, pointing us to a hope that endures, sustains, and overcomes."

> — **Jeff Henderson**
> pastor, Buckhead Church

"I most appreciate this book for its honesty. Pete Wilson avoids the easy answers that we all have heard about suffering. With real-life stories, the wisdom of Scripture, and an authentic search for the redeeming dimension of tragedy, this book will serve all of us who wrestle with what to do when life doesn't deliver us what we expected."

> — **Nancy Beach**
> Willow Creek Association

"Pete Wilson is a tremendous communicator whose warmth and care for people are evident on every page of this fantastic book. *Plan B* is a powerful resource for the detours of our lives. I wish this book would have been available years ago when some of my Plan As crashed, but I'm so thankful for the wisdom of its pages for my Plan Bs today."

— **Jud Wilhite**
senior pastor, Central Christian Church, and author of *Eyes Wide Open*

"While reading *Plan B*, I cheered, wept, and rediscovered parts of my faith that I'd long given up on finding. Like a conversation with an old friend, Pete Wilson's reflections about God and life are engaging, sensitive, and moving. As far as I'm concerned, if you're working on plan A, *Plan B* is a good prerequisite."

— **Matthew Paul Turner**
author of *Churched* and *Hear No Evil*

"In a generation that faces ever increasing disappointment with life, this book masterfully reminds us that God is at work and turns everything around for good. As you read *Plan B*, you will sense the genuine love and concern from a pastor who cares. Well done, Pete."

— **Chris Hodges**
pastor, Church of the Highlands

"If Plan A for your life isn't working out too well, you're not alone. In this book, Pete Wilson helps you make sense of life's frustrations and disappointments. The stories in *Plan B* remind you once again that God, who began a good work in you, is faithful to complete it."

— **Robert Emmitt**
senior pastor, Community Bible Church

Plan B

What Do You Do When God Doesn't Show Up
the Way You Thought He Would?

Pete Wilson

THOMAS NELSON
Since 1798

NASHVILLE   DALLAS   MEXICO CITY   RIO DE JANEIRO

Published in Nashville, Tennessee, by Thomas Nelson. Thomas Nelson is a registered trademark of Thomas Nelson, Inc.

Thomas Nelson, Inc. titles may be purchased in bulk for educational, business, fund-raising, or sales promotional use. For information, please e-mail SpecialMarkets@ThomasNelson.com.

Page design: Walter Petrie

Library of Congress Cataloging-in-Publication Data

Wilson, Pete.
    Plan B : what do you do when God doesn't show up the way you thought he would? / Pete Wilson.
      p. cm.
    Includes bibliographical references.
    ISBN 978-0-8499-4650-9 (pbk.)
      1. Consolation. 2. Disappointment—Religious aspects—Christianity. 3. Suffering—Religious aspects—Christianity. 4. Trust in God—Christianity. I. Title.
BV4905.3.W55 2010
248.8'6—dc22   2009045911

Printed in the United States of America

10 11 12 13 14 RRD 8 7 6 5 4

To all who choose to believe,
in the midst of their Plan B,
that one day faith will win over doubt,
light will win over darkness,
love will win over hate,
and all things will be redeemed
and exist the way they should.

CONTENTS

ACKNOWLEDGMENTS

To Brandi, Jett, Gage, and Brewer . . . I love each one of you more than life itself. I can't imagine the journey without you guys. Thanks for your patience, love, and support through the early mornings and late evenings.

To my Cross Point Church family . . . thank you for allowing me to serve you. You've created a community where everyone's accepted, nobody's perfect, and anything is possible. I love being your pastor.

To the Cross Point staff team . . . where do I start? It's such an honor to wake up every day and work with such an awesome group of all-stars. I wouldn't be in ministry today if it wasn't for you confronting and redeeming my desire to give up!

To Maurilio Amorim and Shannon Litton . . . thanks for your wisdom, faith, and dedication to this book. We all know *Plan B* would never have made it to this point without you.

To Anne Christian Buchanan . . . thanks for adding your gift with words to this book. You continuously challenged me to be a better writer.

To Mike Hyatt and my entire team at Thomas Nelson: Matt Baugher, Dale Wilstermann, Emily Sweeney, Kristi Johnson, Stephanie

Newton, Paula Major, Sally Hofmann, Rick Spruill, Gary Davidson, Mark Schoenwald, and David Moberg . . . thank you guys so much for believing in me and giving me this amazing platform to share this important message.

ONE REALITY

Do you remember the day you discovered your life wasn't going to turn out quite the way you thought?

It happens to everyone sooner or later.

All of us have had dreams, wishes, goals, and expectations that, for a variety of reasons, have not come to fruition.

Plans fizzle. Expectations come to nothing. Trusted people let us down—or we let ourselves down. Dreams shatter or slip away.

Has it happened to you?

Plan A comes to an abrupt stop, and you're not sure if there even is a Plan B.

Maybe the realization hits you in the form of illness or even death—a terrifying diagnosis, a sudden descent into the world of hospital beds and IVs, the sudden loss of a close friend or family member. Maybe it involves a disillusioning church experience or a financial reversal.

Or maybe your shattered dreams come with divorce papers. You expected to finish your life with the partner you married. But your marriage is ending, and you're hurt and disappointed.

I recently met with a woman from our church who had been "happily" married for almost twenty-five years. Three days before our meeting, she had found an e-mail that caused her to start questioning her husband. Over the next several hours, he confessed to a sex and porn addiction that included dozens of affairs over the past twenty years. I'll never forget the look on that woman's face as she sat in my office mourning the betrayal of her trust and the devastation of her dreams.

But your broken dream may be completely different. Maybe, like my friend Dana, you just knew you would be married by now and have a family, but it's just not happening. Dana desperately wants to meet the man of her dreams. On several occasions she thought she had met *the one*, only to be disappointed. Now every wedding she attends is a reminder that life isn't turning out the way she expected.

Keith and Sheila feel the same way when they receive a birth announcement or shower invitation. Their first Sunday at Cross Point Church, where I pastor, they asked me to pray with them. They desperately wanted to have a child, but for some reason Sheila couldn't get pregnant. That was four years ago. Despite continued prayers and several procedures, they are still without a baby.

Do you have a career dream that keeps being frustrated? Maybe you trained as an engineer, but the economy is bad, and no one is hiring. You are convinced God wants you to go into ministry, but no doors are opening up. You were sure you were destined for the corner office, but you're stuck in the cubicle. You've always wanted to be your own boss, but you just can't get a business off the ground.

Or you might be like my friend Brian. He's a great guy that has so much to offer to people around him. He really wants to be involved with ministry in some way, but he wrestles with a drug addiction. Brian has been through several treatment centers and regularly attends twelve-step meetings, but every day is still a struggle. "You know what, Pete?" he told me recently over lunch, "I'm never going to do what I want to with my life because of this problem. I've prayed and prayed and prayed. Why won't God take this addiction away from me?"

Sometimes our disappointments are clearly our fault—we made

a poor decision or took the wrong path. Sometimes another person's poor decisions are to blame. Sometimes, honestly, it's a little of both.

And then there are the times when life just seems to suddenly fall apart with no explanation. It seems totally random.

I was watching a movie the other night—one of those suspenseful, edge-of-your-seat films. I'm not a big fan of that kind of movie because they tend to stress me out. But at least the movies give fair warning when something terrible is about to happen. The camera angles shift, the music grows sinister, a shadow looms. Something tells you, "Watch out."

Don't you wish life was this way? But it's not, is it? It's not even close. Because often our dreams seem to shatter when we least expect it. There's no warning. You can't explain it, you can't blame it on someone else. It just happens, another painful reminder that life can often be unexplainable.

It Happens to Everyone

If you're like so many people I know, your shattered dreams may have left you wondering if God is still actively involved in your life. You may wonder if he even cares or if you're too broken and bruised to be healed by him. You probably wonder quite a lot about what to do next.

No matter what has happened or how you feel, please know you're not alone. Because here's what I'm learning: everyone needs healing. Everyone.

Everyone has shattered dreams.

Every one of us has been let down and disappointed in one way or another.

And every one of us needs healing for our brokeness.

Everyone.

We all have this picture of the way our lives should be. And for some of us the picture of the way our lives should be and the picture of reality is just a reminder our lives are not turning out the way we had hoped.

No matter what has happened or how you feel, please know you're not alone. Because here's what I'm learning: everyone needs healing. Everyone.

We all have dreams, little or large. We all have expectations, reasonable or unreasonable. We all have this mental picture of the way our lives are going to be.

Isn't that true for you? In your mind you probably had it all planned—where you would go to school, whom you would marry, what your kids would be like, what kind of work would bring you satisfaction and purpose. Maybe you dreamed of the perfect house, perfect spouse, perfect two-point-three kids, perfect job. Maybe you saw yourself traveling the world or spending your life in service. Maybe you just hoped to be safe and reasonably comfortable.

Whatever you wanted for your life, if you're a Christian, you may well have assumed God wanted it for you as well. You might not admit it, even to yourself, but you were pretty sure God was going to sweep down and provide for you as only God could do.

The problem is, what you assumed was not necessarily what happened.

Nobody ever grew up thinking, *I'm going to get cancer at forty-one.* Nobody ever grew up thinking, *I'm going to get fired at fifty-seven.* Nobody ever planned to be divorced twice by forty-five or alone and depressed at age thirty-five. Nobody thought their child would end up in prison at age twenty.

You never imagined you wouldn't physically be able to have

children. You never imagined you'd get stuck in a dead-end job. You never imagined the word that might best describe your marriage would be *mediocre*.

But it happened, and you're frustrated. Or hurt. Or furious. Or all of the above.

And let's be honest for a minute. Part of what brings up such strong emotions is the fact that it feels like all the other people around you are achieving their dreams. Their lives seem so put together.

Everyone else is getting married. Everyone else is having kids. Everyone else is successful. Everyone else is healthy. Everyone else is happy in their marriages—or content and productive in singleness.

Does this sound familiar to you at all?

If it doesn't, it will eventually. Because as I have said, it happens to everybody.

So what do you do with a shattered dream? What do you do with an unmet expectation? What do you do when your life isn't turning out the way you thought life was going to turn out?

What do you do when you have to turn to Plan B?

That's what I want to explore in this book.

Because, to tell the truth, I need the answers as desperately as you do.

Grace

I would never pretend to know what you're going through. I would never assume that I understand the pain or confusion you may be experiencing. But I have personally experienced shattered dreams—I'll tell you about a few later. And I've walked with a countless number of people through unspeakable loss.

I planted my first church in Morgantown, Kentucky, just a few months after graduating from college. Not that I have a clue what I'm doing these days, but back then I was absolutely lost! I knew

God had called me to start the church, but I had never been a pastor, and I was only twenty-one years old. I had begun to work my way through seminary, but no seminary could ever fully prepare me for what I would experience as a new pastor.

Morgantown Community Church, although growing fast, was still a fairly small church the first few years I was pastor. The small size was a great fit for me because it allowed me to spend a lot of time with the people in our church. And some of my favorite people in that church were Dan and Kimberly Flowers. The church was only a year or so old at the time, and they had been there almost from the beginning. They were the perfect volunteers. They spent countless hours serving and were willing to do anything that was needed.

Then, all of a sudden, Dan and Kimberly just seemed to disappear. We didn't see them for several weeks. I called one afternoon to check up on them, and they invited me out to their house. They said they wanted to explain to me why they had stopped attending MCC. And they did. That night, over dinner, they very nervously told me they felt they couldn't come back to church because their unwed twenty-year-old daughter, Kelly, was pregnant.

That dinner was just the beginning of a sweet experience of grace for the Flowers family and our entire church. I told Dan and Kimberly that not only would they be welcomed back at MCC, but that nothing would make me happier than to see Kelly get involved as well.

They took me at my word. And I was so proud of our congregation over the next several months as they willingly and generously reached out to that family. Week by week as Kelly's pregnancy progressed, I could see her life being transformed by the love of God's people.

One of my proudest moments as a pastor was showing up one Saturday afternoon at the church office to get a little work done, only to walk in on a group of women holding a baby shower for Kelly. They were laughing and crying together, doing their absolute best to help. Most of the women in that room couldn't have been more different from Kelly. And yet they were extending a love that was beyond themselves.

The highlight of the shower was a beautiful white dress with little pink flowers that one of the women had bought. Kelly was so excited. She immediately squealed, "This is the dress she's going to wear home from the hospital."

I remember getting into my car that afternoon thinking, *This is what God's church is all about!*

Since I had walked the path with this family, I asked Kimberly if she would please call me when Kelly went up to the hospital to have the baby. When the call came, I rushed out to the hospital, which was located about thirty minutes from our small town. I sat in the hallway waiting with Dan. I'm not sure which of us was more nervous. This was Dan's first grandchild, and it was my first time as a pastor walking a church member through this process.

While we sat there chatting, Dan asked me if I knew what Kelly had named the baby. He went on to tell me she had chosen to call the baby Grace, and he thanked me for everything the church had done to show God's love to Kelly. I just sat there in total amazement at everything God had been doing through our church and this family.

But then I started to notice an unusual amount of traffic going in and out of Kelly's room. And all of a sudden, Kimberly stuck her head out the door. "Please pray," she begged. "Something is terribly wrong."

My heart started to beat fast, and my hands got a little shaky. *What could possibly be going wrong? She's just having a baby.* For the next ten minutes Dan and I just sat there, not saying a word but praying like never before.

When Kimberly came out again, she was crying uncontrollably. She finally calmed down enough to tell us that Kelly's baby had been stillborn. Apparently the umbilical cord had wrapped around the baby's neck. Despite the doctors' best efforts, they had not been able to resuscitate little Grace.

I would like to tell you in that moment I stepped up to the plate and did something really pastoral—quoted Scripture, perhaps, or led the family in a prayer. But I didn't. No words came to my mouth. No pastoral thoughts popped up in my mind. I just stood there in silence and watched Dan and Kimberly cry and hold one another.

Then Kimberly said those words that still make me nervous to this day when I think about the moment. She said, "Pete, Kelly would like to see you."

I remember thinking, *Like now?* I wanted to come up with an excuse and take off. I wanted to run and hide. I just knew I couldn't go in there. I didn't know what to say. I didn't know what to do.

I walked into the room completely ill prepared for that moment. I still remember how dark it seemed. There were no noises except for a faint beeping coming from one of the monitors. Most of the medical personnel had cleared out. And there was Kelly sitting on the bed, holding Grace.

I sat by her bed as she kept stroking the baby's head, speaking to her little girl as if the baby's lungs were full of air and the little heart was beating. After about an hour she looked at me with big tears in her eyes and simply asked, "Why?"

I didn't know what to say, so I didn't say anything.

"It just doesn't make sense," she added. "After all God has done over these past few months to restore my relationship with my parents and to show me who he is, why would it all end like this?"

I never answered her question that day—mainly because I didn't have a good answer. As I sit here almost twelve years later, I still don't know that I have a good answer.

I think we all have questions that plague our minds. For many people it's the basic question of "Does God exist?" I don't wrestle too much with that one. In my opinion there is too much evidence of God's existence for me to spend very long questioning it.

No. The question that resurfaces for me again and again and again has more to do with all the unexplainable pain and hurt in this world. The greater struggle for me is that God does exist, yet so does a lot of pain and suffering. There are so many Kellys in this world. So many broken dreams. And while I've spent a lot of time studying and pondering, I have to be honest and say I'm still not sure I understand why.

The question that resurfaces for me again and again and again has more to do with all the unexplainable pain and hurt in this world. The greater struggle for me is that God does exist, yet so does a lot of pain and suffering.

I stayed with Kelly and her parents the rest of the afternoon. There was very little conversation. Most of the time, we just sat there, silently praying and staring at one another in disbelief.

At one point Kelly decided she wanted to dress Grace before the funeral home came to pick up the body. They took the baby away in that pretty little white dress with the tiny pink flowers.

I cried the whole way home that night. I cried because I hurt for Kelly and her family. I cried because I didn't feel like praying. I cried because I couldn't understand why God would allow this.

Three days later, a handful of pallbearers would follow me carrying a little wooden casket up a hill where we would bury baby Grace. As we walked toward the hundreds of people gathered around that gravesite, I wondered, *How am I going to explain this to my church? How do I tell them God didn't show up!* The following question would haunt me for months: What do you do when God doesn't show up for you in the way you thought God was going to show up?

In a way, those questions still haunt me. But I've learned a few things since then that have helped. I've learned a few more things about the Plan Bs of life, mostly through spending time with people in the Bible who faced their own shattered dreams.

The Journey

I'm not sure where you are with your faith. You may not have a relationship with God. You may not believe in the Bible. But if that's true, I'm going to ask you to do me a favor. I'm going to ask you to suspend your judgment. I'm going to ask that you remain open-minded throughout this journey we take together, even though we'll be spending some time in the Bible. You might be surprised where you end up.

On the other hand, you may have grown up in the church. Maybe you've read the Bible all your life, but you've still reached a point where what you thought you knew doesn't seem to be working anymore. You're confused, lost, and possibly annoyed because God hasn't seemed to deliver the way so many over the years have promised you he would. I'm praying this journey provides a new perspective on the promises of God. I'm praying you won't jump to the end of some of these stories you've heard a million times, but will read with fresh eyes.

You know, I've never heard of anyone's journey of faith that hasn't had a Plan B story—a time in life when a person was going through something completely unexpected. A time when she felt as if God were a long, long, long way away if he existed at all.

Those were the times when the stories of Scripture suddenly became very personal.

So maybe, just maybe, there is some wisdom in these ancient Scriptures that could help you answer the "What now?" question. Maybe there are some truths that will unlock hope in your life once again. Maybe there is a way of life you've yet to discover.

I once read a statement that really struck me: "If you don't change your beliefs, your life will be like this forever. Is that good news?"[1]

Think about that for a second. Why did you pick this book up? Why did your friend give it to you?

You're probably at a critical crossroads in your life where you're trying to answer the "What's next?" question or the "Why is this happening?" question. One thing you probably realize is something has to change. You need some answers. You need to change some patterns. Your hope needs to be renewed.

So who knows? Maybe this book could be the catalyst for you. The Bible is full of stories about everyday men and women whose plans didn't work out. It's full of people who were trying to figure out what to do with a life that wasn't turning out the way they expected.

People like you.

People who really needed hope in the midst of a Plan B.

TWO DON'T RUN

While the Bible is full of stories about men and women facing a shattered dream, none are quite as exciting to me as the story of David in the Old Testament. Ever since I was a small child, the story of David has drawn me in.

Just in case you're not familiar with this story, let me pull back and set it up for you. It begins in the book of 1 Samuel, chapter 16.

A Dream Is Born

While David is still a teenager, a man named Samuel shows up at his house one day. Samuel is a prophet sent there by God to pick the next king. He's been instructed by God that the new king will be one of Jesse's sons. Interestingly enough, he picks David. Following God's instructions, he anoints the young man with oil and proclaims he will be king.

This seems kind of strange to David and his entire family because there is already a king named Saul, and everyone assumes that when Saul dies his son Jonathan will take over. Beyond that, Samuel's choice just doesn't add up. David is the youngest and smallest in his family—a kid who herds sheep. Definitely not king material.

And yet, on the day Samuel visits David, a dream is born in the boy's soul. Up until this time his aspirations were probably simpler. He probably hoped he would be a good son. He probably assumed he would work his way up and be promoted from watching sheep to some other blue-collar-type job. But now he has a new dream— the dream of leading his people. After all, a prophet of the Lord said he will be king one day. And David feels different inside—something changed when Samuel anointed him. He feels God's presence in a way he never did before. According to 1 Samuel, the Lord's Spirit starts working in David that very day.

But nothing else changes—not right away. Nothing happens for a long time. And maybe David begins to wonder if Samuel's prediction will ever really come true. I mean, for heaven's sake, he's still out there in the sheep pasture. Now, I don't know if you've ever herded sheep. I personally have not, but I can only imagine it has to be one monotonous job.

You've had doubts like David's, right? You developed certain plans and expectations over your lifetime, and as time went by you started to wonder if any of them would become a reality. Maybe you started to get discouraged. Maybe you started to lose hope. Maybe you're feeling stuck and a little bored.

I'm pretty sure David's feeling that way around the time he goes out to where the Israelites are fighting the Philistines.

He's not a soldier. In fact, the only reason he is going to the battlefield is to take some food to his brothers. When he arrives, he starts to hear about this giant named Goliath who strikes fear in the entire Israelite army. David is young and maybe a little overconfident, and he still has that strong sense that God is with him. He decides to take the giant on himself. And he ends up killing Goliath by hitting the giant in the temple with a stone from his slingshot.

Instantly, David becomes a national hero. He goes from nobody-shepherd-boy to everybody-knows-him hero. King Saul commends him and appoints him to a high-ranking post in the army. He then rewards David by saying, "I would like you to marry my daughter."

David has to be thinking about Samuel about now: *Maybe the old dude was right. Maybe I really am going to become king. I was, like, just a shepherd boy, and now I'm a national hero. The king loves me, and he wants me to marry his daughter. God is definitely doing great things for me. Maybe I do have a shot at this after all.*

Let me pause for a second here because I don't want you to just listen to this story. I want you to interject yourself into these circumstances—because you've been there. You have been in that place where it seems like everything is falling into place. All the circumstances are lining up, and it looks as if your dream just might become a reality.

You get the promotion.

You meet the guy of your dreams.

The pregnancy test comes back positive.

Your spouse agrees to go to marriage counseling.

There is some kind of circumstantial shift that shines a bright light on your hidden dreams and allows your hope to escalate.

Living in Nashville, I have the opportunity to pastor a lot of musicians. It's one of the things I love about my city. It's full of dreamers. People move here from all over the world to chase their dreams, and their hopes are often contagious.

There was a particular band I had the opportunity to spend a lot of time with several years ago. The band members really felt God had given them a purpose. They were extremely gifted and focused, and they seemed to be poised for greatness. They had faithfully toured and practiced and done everything humanly possible to prepare for their big break.

Finally it happened. They signed the promising record contract. They had the right people around them. All circumstantial indications were that God had finally provided the breakthrough they needed. I loved their attitude. They were convinced God had finally opened the door and were prepared to give him all the glory. They recorded an awesome album full of thought-provoking, God-engaging songs.

But nobody ever heard it. The label executive that signed them, believed in them, and pushed them was fired, and they got buried.

Can you imagine how they felt? They'd been so sure that God was finally preparing them for the dream to be achieved.

That's exactly where David is at this point in his story. Up to now, I'm not sure he's even staked a lot of hope in the whole becoming-a-king dream. But now, he begins to think it really might happen.

I suspect something has probably changed in David during this time. His dream has actually become a goal. In his mind, the possibility of becoming king has transformed into a reality. He just knows that God's about to make it happen.

When You Run

But then things start to change. David's not sure what the deal is, but something about King Saul is different. It's little things at first—a roll of the eyes, an annoyed glance. Little hints that the king isn't entirely happy with his homeboy David.

Then one day there's a Jerry Springer-type moment. Saul throws a spear at David, and David's fears are substantiated. Even if you're not relationally perceptive, getting a spear thrown at you is a pretty good clue that something's wrong.

And something *is* wrong. Very wrong. David has been getting way too popular, and Saul has grown overly jealous and bitterly angry.

Jonathan, Saul's son, has become good friends with David. So he comes to him and basically says, "Dude, my dad wants to kill you. He's going to do whatever it takes to get rid of you. You have to get out of here!"

In a matter of minutes, David senses his dream of becoming king is slipping away. Fearing for his life, he does what so many of us have done when we felt our dreams slipping away. He runs. Before Saul knows he's gone, David is out of the country.

On the surface, this might seem a sensible course of action. If someone is trying to kill you, you get out of town, right? You run as fast and as far as you possibly can. But I believe something else is happening in this situation. I believe David is running because he's given up on God.

Remember, from the time Samuel anointed him, David has felt God's presence in a special way. Up to this point, he's been confident God was working in his life. He believed God was going to make him king. But now, when everything seems to be going wrong, David seems to be losing faith that God will fulfill his promise.

So what does David do? He does exactly what many of us have done in such a situation. He panics. He turns his back on God and he tries to take things into his own hands.[1]

In the book of 1 Samuel, as we see David on the run, there is no mention at all of God's presence. I imagine David has very little sense that God is with him. I doubt he feels his dream has any chance of happening. He might even assume God has been toying with him, allowing him to get so close, only to slam the door in dramatic fashion.

Isn't it true we often assume the road to a God-given dream is going to be smooth and lined with lace? As far as we know, Samuel's instructions to David were simply, "One day you will be the king." Apparently he forgot to mention this whole deal about the current king trying to kill David in the process. I'm thinking that information might have been quite helpful.

You see, I believe David is making a huge mistake—the same mistake so many of us have made throughout our lifetimes. He assumes he understands God and his ways. He thinks he knows what God should be doing. And when God doesn't handle things the way he expected, David just gives up.

There is a very important lesson here for every one of us. We get ourselves into all kinds of trouble when we assume God must think and feel as we do.

Someone once said, "Adversity introduces a man to himself." Unfortunately, more often than I like to admit, I have found this to be true. And I cringe when I look back on how I've acted during times when it felt as if God was not there and the bottom was dropping out.

When I was twenty-one, for example, I felt God leading me to start a church. So a couple weeks after I graduated from college, I did just that.

We get ourselves into all kinds of trouble when we assume God must think and feel as we do.

Now, you may be thinking, *How in the world can a twenty-one-year-old kid plant and pastor a church?* I had no formal training, but I had read Rick Warren's *The Purpose-Driven Church*, and I figured that was all the training I needed. So I put together a team, and we got busy. We prayed a lot, had a lot of meetings, even designed an official church logo. Then we launched the church.

On our first Sunday, other than some family and friends who showed up to support us, we really only had one guest. One guy named Gary. This was not exactly the way it had happened for Rick Warren, so I was a bit confused. I'd really expected hundreds would show up. I mean, why wouldn't they? We had prayed for that. We believed for that. We had a band!

But it just didn't happen.

I was so ready to quit, ready to throw in the towel. I wanted to start a church, but I wasn't ready to deal with the disappointment and adversity that would come along with giving birth to this dream.

I honestly don't know if I would have hung in there those first few months if it had not been for the accountability and encouragement of our core team. Looking back, I'm embarrassed at how quickly I would have bailed on the dream. Looking back, I'm ashamed of my desire to run when it felt as if God was not there.

Because after a while, it became clear that God was indeed there. Our whole team persisted, and an authentic, Christ-centered community was born. It was the same church that later showed such love to Dan and Kimberly and Kelly. God did great things through that community. And I'm grateful that with the help of my team I managed to stick out those early days. I'm grateful that instead of running I gave God a chance to do what he'd promised.

Desperation

But back to David. If you read on in the story of David (1 Samuel 21), you'll learn that after fleeing Saul he ends up in a town called Nob, where he meets a priest by the name of Ahimelech, who has no idea what is going on with Saul. In fear and desperation David tells Ahimelech several lies hoping that he will help him out. He lies about what he's doing in Nob. He lies about being on the run. He lies about the state of his spiritual life. And, of course, all that lying is just another form of running. It's using manipulation to get out of a tough situation instead of relying on God to work things out.

Then David tells one more lie. And it's in the midst of this lie that God provides him with a moment he totally misses.

> David asked Ahimelech, "Do you have a spear or sword here? The king's business was very important, so I left without my sword or any other weapon." The priest answered, "The sword of Goliath the Philistine, the one you killed in the Valley of Elah, is here. It is wrapped in a cloth behind the holy vest. If you want it, you may take

it. There's no other sword here but that one." David said, "There is no other sword like it. Give it to me." (vv. 8–9)

Do you see what's happening here? Though David has given up on God, God has not given up on David. He has placed a reminder of his faithfulness right before David's eyes, and David's about to miss it.

The sword that Ahimelech offers him should have served as a wake-up call for David. It's the sword of Goliath, the giant David killed as a mere shepherd boy. It's an icon of God's faithfulness to David. David should look at it and be instantly reminded of what God has done for him, how far God has brought him. He should think, *What am I doing? Why am I running? Why am I lying and deceiving and taking matters into my own hands instead of trusting God?*

But he doesn't. He grabs the sword and does exactly what so many of us do in the midst of our shattered dream. He keeps on running, panicked, from one hideout to another, with Saul right on his heels.

John Quincy Adams once said, "Patience and perseverance have a magical effect before which difficulties disappear and obstacles vanish."[2] There is a lot of wisdom in that statement. And yet in the midst of our chaos we usually do the opposite. We run like crazy.

I remember doing that in the days after baby Grace died. Those were difficult days not only for Kelly and her family but for our entire church. And while I won't speak for everyone in the church, I can tell you that I definitely ran. No, I didn't flee to another country like David did. But in my heart I was running away from the pain and uncertainty of the situation. In a way, I was running from God. I continued to talk about God because it was kind of my job. But I didn't engage him. I didn't seek him out. In fact, I spent the next several months preaching about a God I didn't know if I trusted anymore.

There were several times during those months when God used scriptures, messages, songs, and circumstances to remind me of his faithfulness throughout my life, but I refused to listen. Like David, I learned that deep hurt and shattered dreams have a way of blinding us to the character and beauty of God.

Sadly, I wasn't the only one running in those days. Not long after baby Grace's death, her mother, Kelly, started getting into drugs. Almost six months later I found myself driving around with Kimberly in the middle of the night, looking for Kelly. She had not been home for days. We found her at about three in the morning, passed out in someone's house. We loaded her into the backseat of my car and drove her home. When I last heard from her, Kelly's running had become a full-blown addiction.

The point is, when we give up on God, we easily fall into harmful behavior that hurts ourselves and others. All we can think of is easing our discomfort, leaving the pain behind. Addiction is just one of the ways we tend to run. Peter Scazzero points out others:

> In our culture, addiction has become the most common way to deal with pain. We watch television incessantly. We keep busy running from one activity to another. We work seventy hours a week, indulge in pornography, overeat, drink, take pills—anything to help us avoid the pain. Some of us demand that someone or something (a marriage, sexual partner, an ideal family, children, an achievement, a career, or a church) take the loneliness away. Sadly, the result of denying and minimizing our wounds over many years is that we become less and less human, empty Christian shells with painted smiley faces. For some, a dull, low-level depression descends upon us, making us nearly unresponsive to all reality.[3]

How About You?

So I've got to ask: What do *you* do? What is your pattern when it looks like your dreams are not going to come true? What happens on the inside of you when you give in to panic and start running?

Do you start to lie and manipulate to get what you need like David did?

Do you turn to anger to get what you want?

Do you reach for the bottle or pop some pills or load up on carbs?

Do you retaliate?

Turn your back on God?

More important, where has your running brought you? Did it end your pain or just make things worse?

Let me tell you how this part of the story of David ends. King Saul finds out that David has been in Nob. He finds out that Ahimelech has fed David and armed him. And Saul is furious. It doesn't matter to him that David lied to Ahimelech and manipulated him. It doesn't matter that Ahimelech thought David was still in Saul's good graces; Saul just wants revenge. So he has Ahimelech killed. He also slaughters the other eighty-five priests in Nob and all their families!

And David's ultimately responsible for all that slaughter. He admits as much in 1 Samuel 22. Yes, Saul was cruel and maybe a little crazy. But if David hadn't lied to Ahimelech, it wouldn't have happened.

Stripped

I think it's fair to say this is a low point in David's life. He's been stripped of almost all things dear to him. As Chuck Swindoll puts it,

> David had a position and he lost it. He had a wife and he lost her. He had a wise counselor and he lost him. He had a friend and he lost him. He had self-respect and he lost it. Not unlike Job, it hit him with such back-to-back force, his head must have spun for hours.[4]

Here's something I've learned from this page in David's life and from my own experience. When it becomes apparent your dreams are not coming true and you feel you've been stripped of everything, this is no time to run. It's no time to take things into your own hands. It's definitely not the time to turn your back on God.

This is when you need God more than ever before. You need to lean on him instead of running away.

Your dreams may not be happening, and things aren't turning out the way you expected, but that doesn't mean your life is spinning out of control. It just means *you're* not in control. It's in those moments you can learn to trust the only one who has ever had control in the first place.

Now, I would never wish this on you, but there will be a moment in your life when you feel like everything you have is starting to slip away. You will be tempted to run, but I pray instead you will persevere. Because no matter how things seem, God is still with you. And things will turn around, one way or another. Maybe not the way you planned. Maybe not the way you assumed God would handle it. Maybe not even the way you hope. But you will see God's hand at work—if not in your circumstances, then certainly in your heart.

Your dreams may not be happening,
and things aren't turning out the way you expected,
but that doesn't mean your life is spinning out of control.
It just means *you're* not in control.

It happened for David. It took awhile, but eventually he *did* become king. It happened after he started listening to God again. Even while he was still physically hiding from Saul, he stopped running from God. He stopped trying to make things happen and just started to trust the one who had placed these dreams in his heart from the beginning.

People in Twelve Step programs often share a saying with one another: "Don't leave five minutes before the miracle happens." In the context of sobriety, this phrase is meant to encourage a struggling addict or alcoholic to hang on, to not give in to temptation because relief may be only minutes away.

C. S. Lewis announced a similar principle in his classic *The Screwtape Letters*, in which the senior demon, Screwtape, educates the junior devil, Wormwood, on how to tempt a human "client." In one particular letter, Screwtape explains the tactic of using a human's fatigue during a time of trial to persuade the man to give up:

> Let his inner resolution be not to bear whatever comes to him, but to bear it "for a reasonable period"—and let the reasonable period be shorter than the trial is likely to last. It need not be *much* shorter . . . the fun is to make the man yield just when (had he but known it) relief was almost in sight.[5]

Now, think about that. How many times has that exact demonic trick been used on you? How many times have you missed witnessing God at work in the midst of your shattered dream because you gave up on him five minutes—or five years—too soon?

I'm not blaming you for giving up. I'm not blaming you for being tempted to run and control what you can't control. If I were in your shoes, I might have done the same thing. In fact, I *have* done the same things.

It happens so easily in a crisis. Our trials of life seem to chip away at us, leaving us exhausted, confused, and vulnerable. We resign ourselves to the fact that things simply are the way they are and there is no hope they will ever be any different. Feeling hopeless, we either run, taking things into our own hands, or we give up instead of waiting on God to act.

If you are going through a difficult time in your life, don't buy into these lies.

I know that persevering isn't easy. I know you want to run. I know you want to give up. I know you want to try to control and maintain what you cannot control or maintain.

Resist the urge.

Try to lean toward God instead of panicking.

Try to trust him instead of running away.

Despite what your current circumstances are telling you, God is for you. He is there. He is working things out for your good.

THREE THE ILLUSION OF CONTROL

Do you remember the first time you realized you weren't in total control of your life? That's a tough one for me and a lot of people.

I think most of us tend to view our lives as one of those marionette puppets. We think we have life by a string. There's a string that runs to our relationships and one to our finances and one to our kids, and we assume that we can make them all do what we want. We assume if we work hard enough and pray long enough, eventually we'll be able to manipulate the circumstances to our benefit.

Trouble is, life doesn't work that way.

The greatest of all illusions is the illusion of control.

Peter Scazzero puts it this way:

I like control. I like to know where God is going, exactly what he is doing, the exact route of how we are getting there, and exactly when we will arrive. I also like to remind God of his need to behave in ways that fit with my clear ideas of him. For example, God is just merciful, good, wise, loving. The problem, then, is that God is beyond the grasp of every concept I have of him. He is utterly incomprehensible.[1]

I'll never forget the first time in my adult life I banged my head against this painful reality.

At the time I had been married to my wife, Brandi, for seven years. For both of us, life had been pretty smooth. We both came from good families. We had been blessed enough to have a good education and great jobs. Life wasn't perfect, but it was pretty good. We were always the couple in small group who had a tough time answering the "How can we pray for you?" question. It seemed as if we were always *fine*.

Brandi and I met at Western Kentucky University, where we dated until we both graduated in 1996. We each landed the jobs we wanted right out of college. We had a great church and great friends. Life was picture-perfect.

The greatest of all illusions is the illusion of control.

We both tend to be planners—Brandi even more than me—and all of our plans had gone just the way we had hoped. We had decided early in our marriage that we wanted to wait four or five years before having our first child. All went according to plan.

When we decided we were ready for a family, we even picked out the month we wanted to conceive so Brandi could deliver at a time of the year that worked best with our schedules. (I told you she was a planner.) Sure enough, she got pregnant the first month we tried. Once again we were blessed, and Brandi gave birth to our first son, Jett.

Almost two years later we were ready to try for baby number two, and once again we had a perfect plan. Brandi got pregnant right on schedule, and since our first child was a boy, we were all hoping baby number two would be a girl. Funny how when life is going just as you planned, you actually begin to believe you can control stuff like the sex of your child.

Our first appointment of the first trimester was completely normal. Everything looked great. It was too early for us to find out the sex, but there was lots of talk about pink.

Our next appointment took a turn none of us were expecting. We went into the ultrasound room we'd visited many times before, cracking jokes about the room temperature and how we couldn't wait to see who the baby looked like.

I'll never forget sitting there looking at that screen, waiting with great anticipation to see this little miracle who was forming in my wife's body. As before, out of nowhere, the baby appeared. I've never been good at being able to identify much on those images, so I usually rely on the ultrasound tech to talk me through it all.

But the tech wasn't talking much. While I can't remember her name, I certainly will never forget her face. I could tell she was concerned. Something wasn't right. And then she said those words that ripped right through us. "I'm sorry, but I can't seem to find a heartbeat."

No, that's impossible! I thought. That wasn't the way things worked for us. That wasn't in the script we were writing called "our life." There had to be a mistake.

The tech called for the doctor, and I can remember praying, "God, please. This can't be happening to us. I know you have the power to make this baby's heart start beating right now. I know you can just blink and it will happen."

I must have prayed that prayer a hundred times in the next five minutes. But nothing changed. The doctor came in and confirmed the tech's suspicion. There was no heartbeat. No life.

We walked out of the doctor's office that day stunned. By that point I had walked other people through tragedies. But this was different. This was my reality.

I found it hard to breathe. I was crushed, hurt, and felt extremely alone. My illusion of control was starting to unravel.

All of a sudden I started to wonder, *What now?*

What do you do when you feel your control is slipping away?

A Second Chance

In 2 Samuel 13–16 we pick David's story back up at a much later time in his life. He's already king. His children are grown, and there is turmoil in his family. His firstborn son is Amnon, who is going to be the next king. However, there's a problem with Amnon. He's fallen in love—or in lust—with his half sister, Tamar. And even back in those days, lusting after your sister was a big no-no.

One day Amnon gets the bright idea to pretend that he's sick so Tamar will take care of him and he can be alone with her. (I wonder where he learned to manipulate situations like this.) Just as planned, Tamar comes to take care of him. And while she's there, while he's pretending to be sick, he rapes her. That's right—rapes her.

Now we really have a problem. After he has ruined Tamar's life, Amnon decides he wants nothing more to do with her. He tells her he never wants to see her again and has her thrown out of the palace. Needless to say, she's devastated.

When word gets to David, he makes a very unwise choice to ignore the entire situation. (He might be a great man of God, but as a parent he has his limitations, to put it mildly.) However, David has another son, Absalom, Tamar's full brother, who can't ignore the injustice. He bides his time, planning out the best way to take revenge on his brother.

Absalom waits a full two years, then throws a big party and invites all of his brothers and sisters. At the party, in front of everyone, he comes up and murders Amnon. He purposefully revenges his sister's rape by publicly murdering Amnon. Then the following week they all appear on Jerry Springer to tell their side of the story. I mean seriously, can you believe this kind of family dysfunction?

Well, Jerry Springer doesn't happen, but a lot of other stuff does.

After the murder, Absalom becomes a fugitive. So now David has a shattered daughter in Tamar. Amnon, his firstborn, is dead. And Absalom, whom David dearly loves, is a murderer on the run.

More years go by, but eventually Absalom returns to Jerusalem and starts to serve as a judge and advisor outside of the city. The Bible says that over time he starts to turn the hearts of the people. He's a leader they like. David the king is busy with all sorts of things and they can't get to him anymore, but Absalom is accessible. Absalom understands them and listens to them. In their minds he's what David used to be.

And Absalom, who is still furious with David for not protecting Tamar, has another plan up his sleeve. With the hearts of the people on his side, he devises an elaborate scheme to overthrow David and become the next king.

When It All Comes Crashing Down

In 2 Samuel 15:13, a messenger comes to David with the news that Absalom's conspiracy is gaining strength. "The hearts of the men of Israel are with Absalom" (NIV), the messenger says.

This has to be a painful moment for David. Remember he has spent his whole adult life preparing for and living out his dream to be the king. This is all he knows. It's not only what he does, but who he is. And in one sentence from this messenger, his entire reality comes crashing down.

Up to now David has managed to ignore all the signs. Up to now he could hope and pray that one day he and Absalom would be reconciled. Up to now he could hope his dream of being king would not be threatened.

But now reality sets in. His son has, in effect, declared war on him. His dream is clearly at risk and will likely shatter.

Do your remember a moment like this—when you could no longer ignore the reality that what you had hoped for was not to be?

This is the moment when your wife tells you the marriage is over and she's called a lawyer. When the school counselor informs you your kid is abusing drugs. When your dream guy says he just wants to be friends or your boss looks you in the eye and says, "I have no other option. Today is your last day." This is the moment the doctor tells you there is nothing he can do.

I just have to picture David quietly sitting alone on his throne, allowing these words to echo over and over in his mind: *Your son is going to war with you. He's going to take over your kingdom. Your son is going to war with you. He's going to take over your kingdom.* He can't ignore reality any longer. He has to make a choice.

So what does David do next? Does he run from the problem as he did when Jonathan shared the news with him about Saul wanting to kill him? Does he lie and manipulate his way out of this as he tried years ago when his dream of being king was threatened? Does he take charge of the situation and start rallying his troops to resist Absalom? Here's what happened:

> Then David said to all his officers who were with him in Jerusalem, "We must leave quickly! If we don't, we won't be able to get away from Absalom. We must hurry before he catches us and destroys us and kills the people of Jerusalem." The king's officers said to him, "We will do anything you say." (vv. 14–15)

This decision comes as a shock to the people around David. They never expected him to just roll over. They thought he would be up for the fight. The old David would have begun strategizing, spinning, working the system. But instead he says, "Pack it up. Let's go. If my son wants the throne he can have it."

Why was David willing to give up his rights to the city? He never actually says so, but I think what happened back in Nob made a lasting impact on him. Hundreds of people were killed because he lied and manipulated the truth. In his frantic attempt to control his circumstances he abandoned many of his core values. He's not willing to do that again. So he peacefully leaves the city and the crown to his ambitious, angry son.

Surrendering Control

But the story doesn't end here.

> Zadok and all the Levites with him carried the Ark of the Agreement with God. They set it down, and Abiathar offered sacrifices until all the people had left the city. The king said to Zadok, "Take the Ark of God back into the city. If the LORD is pleased with me, he will bring me back and will let me see both it and Jerusalem again. But if the LORD says he is not pleased with me, I am ready. He can do what he wants with me." (vv. 24–26)

I don't know if you caught those last words of David, so just in case, let me repeat them for you, "He can do what he wants with me." Those words represent a monumental shift in David's life.

In this moment David is doing more than giving up his throne. He's specifically recognizing the fact God is God and he is not! He's recognizing the reality that all control is simply an illusion and surrender to God is not just the appropriate option but the only option. Just because my will won't be done, he's saying, doesn't mean that *God's* will won't be done. I'm not going to try to control and maintain what I can't control and maintain. This is not the story I would write, but hey, I'm not God. I will abandon my dream, but not my God.

The greatest of all illusion is the illusion of control.

I have to admit that this whole concept of giving up control is really tough for me. Ever since I was a kid I have been very competitive. I like to win. I can remember crying when I struck out in baseball. I cried not because I was sad or even embarrassed. I cried because I was so mad. Things didn't turn out the way I wanted them to turn out. To this day, whether I'm working on something at church or with tools at home, I get very frustrated if I can't get things the way I want them.

I'm not the only one. For years I've counseled with people who struggle with this issue of control.

One person will tell me, "Pete, I don't know why I lose my temper when I'm working on my car or I'm trying to hang a picture and I can't get it the way I want." Another will say, "I can barely hold my temper when the kids do the exact opposite of what I tell them." Husbands and wives will describe "going off" on one another for not driving or doing household chores the "right" way.

You know why these things frustrate and anger us? They're reminders that control is an illusion—and we don't like being reminded of that. We want to control the outcomes in our lives. We want to win if at all possible. We want to be right. We want it done our way. This powerful desire leaks into our marriages, our jobs, our parenting.

And the danger for most of us is that not only are we tempted to think we hold the strings to our life; we really think we get to write the script. We buy into the illusion of control. We keep a death grip on those marionette strings. Letting go of control like David did is a humbling and even painful act.

Humble Pie

Life does have a way of humbling us, doesn't it? I was reminded of that recently during a trip to a video store.

A bit of background. As the pastor of a growing church in Nashville, I am often approached by people on the street who know me. Many of them are part of our congregation or people who have visited our church. The trouble is, it's almost impossible for me to know everyone in the church on sight. So while I generally cherish these brief encounters and conversations, I've developed a habit to avoid the embarrassment of not recognizing someone. I usually approach people with a smile, assuming I know them.

One Sunday evening recently I was driving back to the church to speak at our six o'clock service. I decided to walk into Blockbuster to pick up a video to watch with Brandi later that night. As soon as I walked through the door, a nice Blockbuster employee said, "Hey, Pastor Pete, I really enjoyed this morning's service." I gave him a friendly thanks and made sure I got his name. Around the next corner was another Cross Pointer who shared with me how the church had made a difference in her family's life. That was wonderful to hear. We chatted a little while, then returned to our selections.

A few minutes later, while I was browsing the New Release section, a woman I didn't recognize walked up and said, "Excuse me." I instinctively answered, "Hey, how are you?" and gave her a little side hug. She stared back at me with this who-in-the-heck-are-you look and said, "I was just wondering if you had seen this movie before."

To say I was embarrassed and humiliated would be an understatement. I had just hugged a complete stranger in Blockbuster!

Sometimes we're humbled in humorous situations like that one. Other times the situation is a little more painful—such as what happens after David leaves Jerusalem to his son Absalom.

According to 2 Samuel 16, as soon as David's people are out of the city, Absalom and his men move in and take control. Absalom takes possession of everything that belongs to his father, including the throne. But that's not enough for David's son, who decides to inflict further embarrassment and pain. Even though David has peacefully left the city, Absalom gathers his army and goes out to find David, intending to meet him in battle.

Now, the last thing David wants is to go to war with his son, but Absalom has forced his hand. And David is a great warrior and a brilliant military strategist. He shines in battle even when being forced to defend himself against his own son's army.

David's army crushes Absalom's.

Absalom, against David's command, is killed in the battle.

And David regains the throne.

The victory is bittersweet—David weeps in anguish over Absalom's death. But David is still king. He's retained his throne after all. And he's done it not by manipulation, but by surrender. He had to get to the point where he could say, "Not my dream, not my picture of the way my life should be, but your dream, God."

Your will, God.

Your Options

Here is the deal when it comes to your shattered dreams and unmet expectations. When life doesn't turn out the way you thought it was going to turn out, you may think you're losing control. But the truth is, you never had control in the first place. The only thing you do control is how you respond to your disappointments and your unexpected obstacles. And here you have some options.

You can allow the river of fear, anger, and disappointment to just rage. But you need to know that rage will affect every relationship you touch, every job you have, every plan you dream.

It's just the way things work. The fear, the anger, the disappointment you picked up in college, you carry into your marriage. The fear, anger, and disappointment you picked up in your marriage, you carry into your career. The fear, anger, and disappointment you picked up in your career, you carry into your parenting.

We've all met people who live the rest of their lives bitter after some kind of life experience that didn't turn out the way they wanted it to turn out. They never worked through the pain, and they continue to inflict emotional turmoil on themselves and others.

So that's probably not the best option. But it's certainly an option.

Another possibility is to keep trying harder. You can turn yourself inside-out trying to make things happen. You can keep throwing yourself at your problems, wear yourself out yanking on all those puppet strings. But the truth is, you can pull and tug and tug and pull and still have your dreams dissolve in front of your eyes—perhaps along with some of your most treasured relationships.

But you have yet another choice.

You can get to the place where you can say, "Not my will, but your will. I'm not in control. You are."

If you can do that, if you can leave the puppet strings in the hands of someone who actually knows what he is doing, you'll have a lot better chance of surviving your shattered dreams.

No Words

I learned a little about that in the days and weeks after our miscarriage. Those were difficult times for Brandi and me. As a pastor I've always felt pressure to explain and reassure people that God has a plan. But I just couldn't see how God could work through our situation. I discovered it's a lot easier to counsel someone out of a funk than it is to pull yourself out of the funk.

It was the first time in my life I found myself not being able to pray. I tried. There were just no words, no connection.

During this time I became personally familiar with Romans 8:25–26: "if we hope for what we do not see, we eagerly wait for it with perseverance. Likewise the Spirit also helps in our weakness. For we do not know what we should pray for as we ought, but the Spirit Himself makes intercession for us with groanings which cannot be uttered" (NKJV).

I remember thinking, *Spirit, I need you to pray for me. While I grieve, you pray. While I long for things to be different, you pray. While I wait for hope, you pray . . . because I just can't.*

It took a while. But looking back, I can see it was in that very act of saying "I can't" that I began to heal. I was doing what I've always hated to do, relaxing my grip on the strings, finally relinquishing control. And in the process, I was giving God permission to work in my life.

I suspect that's the real beauty of surrender. Giving up control is difficult and even painful, but it makes room for God to work, healing us from past pain and helping us move forward, hopefully, into a fresh future.

Let It Be

You've probably heard the powerful story that opens the gospel of Luke. It's a story about an angel who brings a message to a young girl from the town of Nazareth. Her name is Mary.

The angel reveals amazing, unbelievable, and probably terrifying news. Though Mary is a virgin, the Holy Spirit will come to her and she will become pregnant. She will bear a son named Jesus, who will really be the Son of God. What's more, Mary's cousin Elizabeth, who is barren and well beyond childbearing age, is already sixth months pregnant.

Needless to say, Mary is overwhelmed by what the angel says. She can barely wrap her mind around it. She has a million questions. Getting pregnant and giving birth to God's Son is not exactly the life she planned. Talk about a change of course!

But here's what Mary says in response to the angel's news: "Behold the maidservant of the Lord! Let it be to me according to your word" (Luke 1:38 NKJV).

Did you get that?

Mary says, "Let it be." And those simple words usher her into a season of wonder.

With these words, she lets go of her plan, her way, her dreams, her expectations, and her will . . . and makes open a channel for God to change the world.

And that's just the beginning.

Mary does give birth to Jesus, who some thirty-three years later will whisper very similar words back to his Father God in the garden of Gethsemane. Facing the ultimate Plan B and wondering if there's another way, he still prays his willingness to surrender control: "My Father, if it is not possible for this painful thing to be taken from me, and if I must do it, I pray that what you want will be done" (Matt. 26:42).

In other words, let it be.

And just see what God can do when you give him room to work.

FOUR YOUR JORDAN

One of the characteristics I have noticed about the Plan B situations in my life is that they often require more of me than I think I have.

This makes sense when you think about it. Generally when we make plans and dream dreams, we draw on our giftedness, our skills, our education. We skew toward our preferences and our comfort zones.

Plan A seems perfect for us. Plan B by definition seems harder and a lot less appealing.

But while I would never desire a shattered dream or wish a major disappointment on anyone, I've discovered that Plan Bs have a good side too. They almost always grant us opportunities to stretch and draw closer to God.

I had breakfast the other day with Will. Will is an amazing entrepreneurial businessman. He's already made more money than most of us will see over the course of our lifetimes.

A couple of years ago, Will had what many would think was the picture-perfect life, with a beautiful wife, three adorable children, and a multimillion-dollar company he had built and was getting ready to sell. Then one day, two weeks before the sale of his company would be final, Will walked into his bedroom and overheard his wife on the telephone. His wife was telling her mother that she was planning to leave him in the next several weeks.

Will was completely blindsided. He'd had no clue she was unhappy, no clue she was getting ready to bail on their twelve-year marriage. And he had never suspected the circumstances that drove her decisions. Apparently Will's wife was having an affair, and she saw the sale as the perfect opportunity to make her move and reap the maximum financial advantage.

Will suddenly was facing a situation unlike any he had ever faced. He knew how to start a company from scratch. He was gifted at making money. But dealing with an unexpected, shattered dream of this magnitude was beyond his experience and his skill set, and he didn't have a clue what his next step would be.

Life can be tough when the rug gets ripped out from underneath you.

The Promise

There is a guy in the Old Testament by the name of Joshua who found himself in one of those stretching situations where he had one plan in his head but God took him in a totally different direction.

Let me catch you up on what's going on when we meet Joshua in the Bible. He's a Hebrew living in the wilderness. His parents' generation was the one God led out of slavery in Egypt. Under Moses' leadership they journeyed toward the promised land, to the place of freedom and plenty God said he would take them. At some point in the journey, Joshua became Moses' assistant. They actually reached the banks of the Jordan River, the boundary of the promised land.

But then things went wrong. There were a series of misfires, if you will, where the Hebrews had a chance to move into this promised land but just couldn't manage it. Fear of the unknown kept them from realizing all God had for them. So for years they wandered around, having a glimpse of the life God had called them to but not quite able to take advantage of it.

While they wandered, the Israelites regularly complained that God was not sufficient. They didn't believe God was really going to enable them to do what he was calling them to do. They constantly grumbled and lived in fear. (I'm sure none of this sounds familiar to you.) Meanwhile, the first generation of Israelites who had left Egypt were dying off.

Then Moses died. The baton of leadership passed to Joshua. God told Joshua it was time to get moving. And that's where we find him at the start of this story. It's his responsibility to finally lead God's people into the promised land.

As Joshua and the new generation of Israelites stand on the banks of the Jordan, God has some important words for them:

> The Lord said, "My servant Moses is dead. Now you and all these people go across the Jordan River into the land I am giving to the Israelites. I promised Moses I would give you this land, so I will give you every place you go in the land . . . No one will be able to defeat you all your life. Just as I was with Moses, so I will be with you. I will not leave you or forget you.
>
> "Joshua, be strong and brave! You must lead these people so they can take the land that I promised their fathers I would give them. Be strong and brave. Be sure to obey all the teachings my servant Moses gave you. If you follow them exactly, you will be successful in everything you do. Always remember what is written in the Book of the Teachings [God's law]. Study it day and night to be sure to obey everything that is written there. If you do this, you will be wise and successful in everything. Remember that I commanded you to be strong and brave. Don't be afraid, because the Lord your God will be with you everywhere you go." (Josh. 1:1–9)

I have to assume that Joshua is prepared to lead the people. He's spent decades as Moses' aide, training for this moment. So nothing

God is saying here is really new to him. God is just giving him a little pregame pep talk: "Joshua, just remember what you know. Be strong. Be courageous. And whatever you do, don't forget I'm with you."

God has a few words for Joshua's people as well: "Don't live in fear. I don't want you to make the same mistake your parents did. Listen to me, pay attention to my instructions, and everything will work out for you."

Finally God makes the whole nation a promise: "If you trust me, if you'll follow me, I'll be with you. Every place you set your foot in that land, I've already gone ahead of you. My power will be available for you. You're not going to undertake the rest of your life on the power of just your own resources."

The Test

That's a great promise. Joshua and the Israelites must have found it extremely encouraging. But then just two chapters later, God gives Joshua some instructions that will put this promise to the test:

> "Now choose twelve men from among you, one from each of the twelve tribes of Israel. The priests will carry the Ark of the Lord, the Master of the whole world, into the Jordan ahead of you. When they step into the water, it will stop. The river will stop flowing and will stand up in a heap." (Josh. 3:12–13)

I can already hear the conversation going on in Joshua's head. *God, you want me to do what? You want me to cross what? I've just taken charge, and now you want me to convince the people it's a good idea to cross the Jordan? When you promised us success, I didn't think it was going to involve this.*

But those are the instructions. God spells out very clearly the next step Joshua and his people must take.

What happens next will become a defining moment in Joshua's life.

At one time or another we all reach this point of decision. But to understand just how big of a decision it is for Joshua, I think it's helpful to understand just a little bit about the Jordan River. It's a very important river in Israel's life.

The Jordan actually starts up around Mount Hermon, and it comes down to the Sea of Galilee and keeps flowing down to the Dead Sea. Mount Hermon, where it starts, has an elevation of about seven thousand feet. It's quite high. The Dead Sea is the lowest body of water on earth, almost thirteen hundred feet below sea level. So the Jordan has quite a descent to get to its destination. Its Hebrew name *Yarden* actually derives from the word *yarad*, meaning "descend."[1]

What's your Jordan River?
What is your Plan B situation? Where is God
asking you to take a seemingly impossible step,
a step of faith?

For Joshua's people, the Jordan River marks both a literal and symbolic boundary. It's what stands between them, on this side, and the life, the land God is calling them to. It's something they have to get across in order to have the future that has been promised to them.

But here's where things start to get a little interesting. Joshua 3:15 tells us that the Jordan is "at flood stage" (NIV) when God gives his instructions. I assume that means all the water from mountain rains is pouring down that long descent, filling the riverbed with very deep, extremely fast-moving water. It's overflowing its banks. There's no bridge. There are no boats—and boats would probably be swept away anyway. And God's telling Joshua to just hoist up the ark of the covenant and step into the flood.

This is Plan B at its finest. Plan A was "let's just walk across the river"—not really easy, but at least possible. It can be done. But Plan B doesn't look too inviting. In fact, it looks downright suicidal.

But that's the point. Because Plan B situations force us to rely on a power beyond ourselves.

That's what Joshua and the Israelites were really dealing with. What was going to be extremely difficult has now become seemingly impossible. They've come all this way, there's the promised land just on the other side of the Jordan, and there's no way to get across. And they wonder what in the world Joshua has done.

What in the world has God done?

I remember talking with Will about the weeks immediately after his wife left him. He describes himself as "a mess"—and understandably so. I'd be a mess too. He said he cried out to God night after night, begging him for another way. He said he kept asking God what he had done wrong. He was full of anger, hurt, and questions, such as "Why is God punishing me?" and "Why has God abandoned me?"

Will would realize later that God was with him. God hadn't abandoned him. Will just couldn't feel God's presence because he was facing one of the biggest emotional barriers of his life. One that would require him to trust in something beyond his own ability.

Like Joshua, Will was facing his own personal Jordan River.

One Step

So what happens next with Joshua?

This might be hard to believe, but even though he and his people face a seemingly impossible barrier, they're exactly where God wants them to be.

Remember the instructions? God has said, "I'm going to make a way. I will allow you to cross the Jordan River. I want you to go down, and you put a foot in the Jordan River, and when you do that, I'll get you across safely."

So picture the Israelites approaching the flooded river, led by a group of priests who are carrying the ark of the covenant, the symbol of God's presence that they've been carrying in the desert their whole lives. I'm sure there were certain days the priests fought over who would get to be in the front but not today. They're walking right towards a deathtrap.

Now, you've got to understand God is teaching his people a huge lesson. (It's a test, remember.)

Israel is facing an obstacle, a barrier, a particularly terrifying Plan B. They've got to get across the Jordan to get to God's life for them. And God has promised that his power is sufficient to make that happen. God will deliver them. God will make a way.

But (and this is a big but) they have to take the first step. They will not see God's power, they will not experience his faithfulness, until they get their feet wet.

God tells them, "I want you to take one step in the Jordan, and then you'll see me at work." He's teaching his people how that trust works.

And here's what happens:

> When the priests carrying the Ark came to the edge of the river and stepped into the water, the water upstream stopped flowing. It stood up in a heap a great distance away. (Josh. 3:15–16)

See, God is teaching his people: I have so much power, and I want to manifest it in your life. But if you want to see my power, you have to take the risk. You have to take the step. You have to take the spiritual risk of trusting me first.

He's teaching us too. We have to take that risk if we're going to live the kind of lives God has called us to live, to be the people God dreamed of when he thought us into existence. So many miss out on this designed life because we make an unconscious vow that we will only trust ourselves and the things we think we can control.

You see, this isn't really about Joshua. It's not about Will. It's about you.

What's your Jordan River? What is your Plan B situation? Where is God asking you to take a seemingly impossible step, a step of faith?

Because here's what I know: everybody faces a Jordan. Every one of us faces a barrier that is keeping us from the life God has for us.

What's Your Jordan?

In May of 2009 I spoke at a missions conference in the Dominican Republic. It was essentially a gathering of pastors from around the Dominican Republic and Haiti. During the day, we had some free time. So I headed down to the beach with Ryan Bult, our church's pastor of missions, who was traveling with me.

That was some beautiful beach—white sand, blue waves, a gentle sea breeze, glorious sunshine. While sitting there just soaking in the beauty of it all, we noticed a woman sitting next to us. She was reading William P. Young's very popular book, *The Shack*. While I hadn't read the book (I think I might be the only Christian left who hasn't), I felt prompted to ask her about it. And that turned out to be an absolute God prompt. She said her name was Karla and that a friend had sent her to the Dominican with that book to help her find healing. Then she started to tell us her devastating story.

Karla had grown up in the church, but her church experience had been a nightmare for her. For almost seven years, from the time she was ten or eleven, her pastor had sexually abused her. The abuse stopped when she was seventeen. By then she had made a choice to turn her back on God, whom she held responsible for all that had happened. She never told anyone about the abuse. And for forty years it continued to take a toll on her life. It damaged her marriage, her relationship with her kids, her ability to make good friends and even keep a job. She was still locked in a horrible cycle of self-hatred, low self-esteem, bitterness, and rage.

I'll never forget what she said to me there on that beach. She looked me in the eye and asked, "Pete, do you really believe there is a loving God in heaven? And if you do, how do you reconcile the fact that he allowed this to happen to me? I just can't believe in that kind of God."

As I've mentioned, I don't have an easy answer to that one. So all I could do was listen. All I could do was care.

Ryan and I spent the next forty-eight hours with Karla—listening, sharing, crying together, and praying. Much of our focus was on her need to forgive the man who had abused her for so many years. She didn't want to do it. She didn't think she could do it. I began to see she couldn't let go of her hatred toward him because she felt that if she did that, he would "get away" with the terrible things he did to her. She felt she was somehow punishing him by holding on to her anger toward him. And yet the only person she was really hurting was herself. She was allowing her abuser to continue to control her.

Plan B situations of all kinds can provide fertile ground for hate and bitterness. It may be focused toward God, or it might be focused toward someone else, someone we blame for our shattered dreams. Either way, the reality is, hate and bitterness are both poisons to the redemptive work God wants to do in and through our lives. And the only way I know to drain the poison is through forgiveness.

At that point, forgiveness had become Karla's Jordan. It was her barrier, the one thing she couldn't muster up the faith to trust God with. And that, in turn, was keeping her from being the wife, mother, and woman God had created her to be.

God's power generally gets released when somebody trusts him enough to obey him.

I'll never forget watching her begin the process of forgiveness that very weekend. You could literally see a change in her physical appearance—she looked as if a weight was being lifted off of her. She was beginning to trust in a loving God once again. She was stepping out in faith and beginning to let go of what had held her back for so many decades.

One of the sweetest moments of my entire life in ministry came while standing in a circle on that Dominican beach, holding hands with Karla, Ryan, and Moise, a Dominican pastor. Ryan and I had been getting ready to catch our plane when Karla asked if we could pray together. (She had never prayed out loud in her life.) So I stood there holding hands with her and my friends as she tearfully asked God to help her begin to forgive the man who had tormented her for so many years. She was stepping out into her Jordan. And the flood was already starting to recede.

So I ask you again: What's your Jordan? What's your barrier? What is keeping you from the future God has for you?

Is it a relationship that's falling apart?

An addiction you can't seem to conquer?

A financial hole you feel you'll never dig yourself out of?

Where is it you're having a hard time trusting God?

I think God's words for Joshua as he stands beside the Jordan are also for each one of us. God says, "I've already gone ahead of you. I'll be there for every step you take; I've occupied the land. But you've got to choose." And because stepping into the Jordan, whatever your Jordan is, always involves overcoming fear, God keeps repeating what he told Joshua over and over again:

"Don't be afraid."

"Don't be afraid."

"Don't be afraid."

The Lesson

God was saying that to Will, too, but it took a while for him to hear it.

He spent the weeks after his wife's departure feeling he could never get out of bed. He spent the next several months wondering if life was worth living. But in those painful weeks and months God was beginning a work in Will's life, and it brought him to the banks of his own Jordan. He realized he couldn't do life on his own. His business savvy and unbelievable success would not be enough to make life work. He had to take the spiritual risk, to start really trusting in Christ against his own instinct. He had to step out into the water.

When he did, he learned the lesson that Joshua and his people also had to learn—that God's power generally gets released when somebody trusts him enough to obey him.

Did you notice how God didn't part the water until the priest put a foot into it? And don't you hate that?

I mean let's be honest. I don't *want* to have to wait until I get all the way into the river for God's power to show up. I don't *want* to have to put my foot in the water. I want God's power when I'm still fifty yards away. Or even better, before I even decide to move. I'd rather be sure.

But that's just not the way it works with faith. We have to move before we're sure. We have to step into the floodwaters while they're still gushing past us. And doing that takes courage.

Million-Dollar Question

So where does the courage come from? That's the million-dollar question, isn't it? How did Joshua manage to be "strong and brave" enough to take God at his word? Why was he able to trust when a lot of other people couldn't?

I want to show you something few people ever notice in Scripture. And this is the one secret you need to know if you want to be the kind of person who can truly trust God in your Plan B situations. It's what you need if you want to be the kind of person who dares to take the step of faith when nothing is certain and all logic says, "Don't do it!"

To see it, we have to go all the way back to the book of Exodus, some forty-five years before Joshua faced his Jordan. The children of Israel were still living in the wilderness, with Moses leading the way. And this is what happened:

> Moses used to take a tent and set it up a long way outside the camp; he called it the "Meeting Tent." Anyone who wanted to ask the LORD about something would go to the Meeting Tent outside the camp. Whenever Moses went out to the Tent, all the people would rise and stand at the entrances of their tents, watching him until he entered the Meeting Tent . . . The LORD spoke to Moses face to face as a man speaks with his friend. Then Moses would return to the camp, but Moses' young helper, Joshua son of Nun, did not leave the Tent. (Ex. 33:7–8, 11)

Make careful note of that last little fact. Long before he became the leader of his people, long before he stood at the Jordan, Joshua spent a lot of time face to face with God. That's why he's able to trust God when others can't. That's why he's able to step out bravely when others are retreating.

He's learned the truth that makes all the difference: constant contact with the Creator is essential for transformation living. If you want faith enough to live the life God's called you to live, time with God is simply a must. And that applies double when you're facing a Plan B situation.

Constant contact with the Creator
is essential for transformation living.

It's so easy to fall into the trap of assuming some people are just more trusting than others. Some people can trust God in the midst of difficulties, and others can't. I don't really believe that. I think that's a cop-out and, for most of us, nothing more than an excuse.

The thing is, trust takes practice. It works better in the context of a prior relationship. (Isn't it easier to trust someone you know?) And while it's possible to muster up faith in the stress of a Plan B situation, it's a lot wiser to lay the groundwork ahead of time.

When we've taken the time to understand God's character, faith comes easier.

When we've experienced his faithfulness, it's easier to be brave.

And the more time we spend in his company, the more ready we are to step forward when he says it's time.

Get Ready . . . Go!

This summer I scratched another item off my "bucket list"—my mental list of things I want to do before I die. I went surfing with my two oldest boys. I had a blast out there in the waves learning to surf. I had even more fun helping the boys learn how to do it.

It took a little while for us to get the hang of it. But eventually we discovered that surfing is all about timing.

If we got too far out in front of a wave, it would wash over us and we'd fizzle out. If we waited too long to get our momentum going, we might miss out on an incredible wave that could take us all the way in. Success for us was completely dependent on watching, being ready, and knowing exactly when to start paddling.

The boys had the most success when I would stand watch for them. They would be ready to start paddling, and I would be looking for the perfect wave for them. When I saw it I'd yell, "Go! Start paddling!" and off they'd go.

It quickly became obvious that two things were essential for the boys to successfully surf a wave.

First, they had to be ready. They had to be properly positioned on the board and watching me, ready to start paddling the minute I gave the word.

And second, they had to trust me for the timing. They had to wait until I said go. And when I said it, they had to paddle. They couldn't hesitate a second.

And that's another secret to faith and courage and trusting God in our Plan B situations. There's timing involved—God's timing.

There have been times in my life that God has sent incredible opportunities my way, opportunities that could move me past my disappointments and frustrations into a whole new way of living. But I simply wasn't ready to move. I wasn't paying attention. My thoughts and my focus were elsewhere. So I missed the wave.

There have been other times when I was ready but too anxious. I wasn't willing to wait on God's timing. So I took things into my own hands, got too far out in front, and wiped out.

I'm learning more and more that if I want God's help in my life, I need to be ready for what he's going to do. I have to be willing to wait for his signal. And when he says go, I'd better start paddling.

That's a good thing to keep in mind in those times when you're swimming around in frustration and disappointment, trying to cope with the loss of your dreams.

You might be terrified. You might be depressed and overwhelmed. You might be wandering aimlessly, not knowing what to do next. But now is the time to watch and wait for what God is going to do.

Because as Psalm 31:15 reminds us, our lives and our times are in God's hands. And when he says go, it's time to go.

When you sense the timing is right, I hope you'll trust his voice.

You just might find that Plan B is the ride of your life!

FIVE PARALYZED

As a pastor I get the chance to spend a lot of time with people who are facing Plan B situations. It's amazing to me the different ways they react. But one of the most common responses I see can best be described with the word *paralyzed*.

People living in the midst of a Plan B often have that deer-in-the-headlights look about them. Maybe this is the first time or the first time in a long time they've faced a situation that is totally out of their control. So they're frozen with fear, incapacitated with worry, so anxious about what has happened and what might happen next that they can't make a choice or a change. Sometimes they can barely breathe.

Fear, of course, is a universal human experience, and it's not limited to Plan B experiences. As far as I can tell, experts disagree about whether we're actually born being afraid of anything. Some say we're born with the fear of falling and the fear of noise. Some add fear of abandonment or even fear of snakes to the list. (I'm quite sure I was born with this fear!) Others deny that any of these fears are innate and insist that all fear is learned.

But there doesn't seem to be much disagreement about the fact that we come into this world with the *capacity* to be afraid. And most of us begin developing fears at an early age.

Are you afraid of the dark? I can remember how darkness terrified me as a child. Now I watch my kids deal with the same fear, especially at bedtime. We follow the same routine every night. I check under their beds and in their closets, assuring them that nothing bad is lurking in the shadows. Then I turn on their nightlights so they don't have to sleep in total darkness.

I'm sympathetic to their fear because while I've learned to live with darkness, I still don't really like it.

And here's the thing. I've come to believe that fear of the dark isn't really fear of the dark. It's more basic than that. What my kids are really afraid of is what most people are afraid of.

What they really fear is the unknown.

We're afraid of what we can't see, what we can't anticipate, what can jump out at us, what can go bump in the night. We're afraid of being disoriented and vulnerable, at the mercy of forces beyond our control. Being in the dark, which usually accompanies a Plan B, reminds us of our uncertainty and inadequacy in the face of all the bad things that can happen to us or those we love.

Inside and Outside the Fence

At our house we have a fenced-in backyard. I believe this is essential when you have three wild boys who love to play outside. Well, let me clarify. What they really love is to play in the dirt. I think if we had lots of dirt in the house they would probably be just as happy playing inside.

When our boys are playing in the backyard, we have a level of comfort as parents. We know they're relatively safe there because inside the fence we can control the variables. We've tried to remove most of the potential weapons—sticks, rocks, crab apples. (Do you know how much damage a crab apple can do when launched at another human being?) We've scouted out the climbing opportunities and digging risks and made sure no poisons are within their reach. We have some say about who enters the yard. It's impossible to guarantee that three active boys will escape occasional cuts and contusions and other problems. But inside the fence we feel they have a better chance.

Inside the fence is known. Outside the fence is unknown.

Now expand this idea to life in general. Most of us have a fence inside our minds. And we think of most experiences and possibilities as either inside the fence (the known, the comfortable) or outside the fence (the unknown, the unpredictable, the frightening—the dark).

You know about that flutter you get in your stomach, the stutter you get in your speech, the sickening feeling you have when you get close to the edge of what feels safe and familiar to you?

Don't you hate that sense of not knowing what's going to jump out at you next? That's fear of the unknown, and like I said, all of us live with a certain amount of it. Most of the time, though, that fear is countered by other forces at work in our minds and hearts, things like curiosity and hope and ambition and positive experiences. When something good happens to us, it tends to cut back our fear of the unknown just a bit. We become accustomed to thinking in possibilities. We *want* to explore the rich world beyond our backyards.

But a negative experience like a disappointment or a betrayal can override all those motivations. Being blindsided hypes our fear of the unknown. It can make us hunker down, not daring to move or take a risk. Hope and faith and curiosity lose their power to move us forward. We're not just fearing the unknown; we're fearing a *bad* unknown. If it happened once, we assume it could happen again.

Training Your Mind

The human brain is an amazing organ. It allows you to think, solve problems, and take care of your daily chores. It handles your heartbeat, your breathing, and the balance that allows you to walk. But your brain has another important function: it serves to keep you safe in the world.

Your brain is literally trained throughout your life to detect danger and to keep you safe. When it perceives a threat, it signals your nervous system and your organs and your muscles to respond—to run, to freeze, to pull away, or to leap into action and fight off danger. Your conscious mind and your emotions come into play as well. All this is designed to help you respond quickly to circumstances that threaten your life and well-being.

In order for all this to work, though, you need to be able to recognize what a threat is. How do you do that? You learn from experience. If a strange dog appears in your yard and bites you, the safety center in your head logs that information: strange dogs are a threat. You also learn from what you observe and what you're taught—to be wary of strangers, concerned about germs, and so forth. Over the course of your lifetime, your brain processes countless experiences and labels them according to the threat they represent.

And this is a good thing. Recognizing threats could possibly save your life—which is the purpose of fear in the first place.

The problem is that your brain doesn't always interpret threats correctly. It can send out false alarms. It can tell you to fear something that isn't really a threat. It can exaggerate the nature of the threat. It can also get stuck on worry and anxiety, fixating on a *possible* threat that may not ever happen.

So while your brain's fear mechanism is there to protect you, it can also be a problem, especially in stressful Plan B times. It can perpetuate feelings of fear that, if trusted, will keep you fenced in a safe little area away from opportunity and growth and the life God has for you.

Fear Is Limiting

Writer and speaker Erwin McManus once said, "Our fears establish the limits of our life."[1]

This is so true, isn't it? If you fear heights, you will tend to stay low. If you fear the outside, you will stay inside. If you fear people, you'll stay alone. If you fear failure, you simply won't try. And when you're under stress, I've observed, this limiting effect is heightened.

So when many of us encounter a Plan B situation—a head-turning crisis or a sudden loss or a significant disappointment—our instinct is to freeze, to become paralyzed. We allow the fear of the unknown to establish the limits of our lives. We can't make decisions, we can't move, we can't grow.

This is definitely not God's will for our lives. In fact, it will most certainly keep us from becoming the persons God envisioned when he thought us into existence.

So what do we do? How do we move beyond our hyped-up fear, our worst-case scenarios, our fervent desire to avoid pain by staying inside a comfortable, predictable fence?

Because our fears stem from what our brains have "learned," the solution has to begin there.

Changing the Patterns

Romans 12:2 reminds us, "Do not conform any longer to the pattern of this world, but be transformed by the renewing of your mind. Then you will be able to test and approve what God's will is—his good, pleasing and perfect will" (NIV).

So what is the pattern of this world? If we look closely, we can probably discern several distinct patterns.

There is the pattern of hurry—*now, now, now, faster, faster, faster.*

There is the pattern of debt—*enjoy now, pay later (if at all).*

But one of the patterns I see every single day in the lives of people I rub elbows with is fear and anxiety. I truly believe there is a pattern of fear in our culture, probably made worse by our constant media presence. We're constantly alerted to possible sources of danger, conditioned to see threats all around us. We're instructed to cover our tails, to trust no one, to avoid failure at any cost. We're especially set up to feel threatened by whatever is outside our fence.

But how do we do break free of these pattern of fear? We've already learned them, right? They're already stored up in our brains. How can our minds be renewed, our fear centers retrained?

Proverbs 3:5 suggests a place to start:

> *Trust the Lord with all your heart,*
> *and don't depend on your own understanding.*

The implication here is that we can't always trust our own minds because they've been trained by the patterns of this world. We can't always trust in the red flags our minds throw. We can't live in the pattern of fear. It's possible, in fact, that God may call us to run in a direction diametrically opposed to where our fearful minds tell us to go.

But that's tricky, isn't it? After all, we still need some fear. We need the messages that warn us of authentic dangers. But we don't need the worry and anxiety that stresses us out and keeps us from really living.

So the trick is relearning what to fear and what not to fear, what's worth worrying about and what isn't. The beauty for those of us who claim to follow Christ is that we can trust in something far more reliable than our own thinking or the thinking of the world around us to help us make those judgments.

The trick is relearning what to fear and what not to fear, what's worth worrying about and what isn't.

A New Perspective

One of Jesus' most brilliant teachings spoke to this very topic. In his famous Sermon on the Mount he addresses the paralyzing worry, fear, and anxiety each one of us tends to experience when confronted with a Plan B experience:

> "So I tell you, don't worry [be anxious] about the food or drink you need to live, or about the clothes you need for your body. Life is more than food, and the body is more than clothes." (Matt. 6:25)

Is Jesus saying you shouldn't be concerned about the fact that you just lost your job, the economy is tanking, your marriage is unraveling, your kids are straying, or your friend is dying? Absolutely not. He's just saying, "I want to give you a different perspective. I want to help you retrain your mind."

I don't know if you've ever had the opportunity to spend time around someone who's facing death. As a pastor I've spent time with plenty of people who have been days or minutes away from leaving this life. The similarity in our conversations is almost uncanny. Dying people almost always talk about how they finally "get it." They understand they've spent too much of their lives worrying about things that weren't worth worrying about and fearing things that just weren't worth fearing. They usually long to have those moments of life back.

Well, I believe Jesus is trying to help us get it. He's not saying we shouldn't be concerned about problems. He's just trying to help us understand what's ultimately important.

"Isn't life more than your car that's broken down?" he's saying. "Isn't it more important than your kids not getting into the school of their choice? Isn't it more important than what happens to your 401k?"

And when we look further he says, "Look at the birds in the air. They don't plant or harvest or store food in barns, but your heavenly

Father feeds them. And you know that you are worth much more than the birds" (v. 26).

Have you ever watched a bird? My friends regularly make fun of my secret bird-watching hobby. I don't know why I like watching birds, but there is something kind of peaceful about it. I know, I know—I'm like an eighty-year-old man trapped in a young man's body. But what I've learned by watching birds is that they really don't do a lot. They just seem to fly from tree to tree, kind of aimlessly going through their day.

Ever had someone call you a birdbrain? It's not a compliment! Truth is, birds are not the brightest animals in the animal kingdom. As a matter of fact, the majority of the space in their little skulls is actually taken up by their eyeballs, leaving very little space for gray matter.

But despite their seeming lack of purpose and intellect, Jesus says God takes care of them. "Hey, look at those birds. If God knows about their problems and challenges, don't you think he knows about yours? Aren't you much more valuable than a bird?"

Now, look at the next verse, where Jesus really cuts to the chase. Get this: "You cannot add any time to your life by worrying about it" (v. 27).

Every time I read that verse, I just have to shake my head. Jesus had this way of putting things that would just stop people dead in their tracks and force them to think about the core of their lives.

Think about what he is saying here, the perspective he's giving us. Can anyone honestly say the time he has spent fearing a Plan B, worrying about the unknown, has added any length or value to his life?

Motivational speaker Earl Nightingale didn't think so. He once famously compared worry to a fog that can keep us from seeing things as they really are. He went on to point out that "a dense fog covering seven city blocks, to a depth of 100 feet, is composed of something less than one glass of water." Categorizing our common worries, he said 40 percent of the things we worry about never happen. An additional

30 percent are things that happened in the past and can't be changed anyway. Needless concern about our personal health occupies 12 percent of our worries, and 10 percent of our worries are petty, miscellaneous items.

In other words, according to Nightingale, "Ninety-two percent of worries are pure fog with no substance at all." That leaves about 8 percent of our worries as legitimate matters worthy of our concern.[2]

Fashioned for Faith

Incidentally, the Greek word translated *worry* that is used throughout this passage in Matthew literally means, "to be drawn in different directions."[3] This is what happens inside our minds when we succumb to patterns of worry and paralyzing fear. We're pulled apart, stretched painfully between the known and unknown.

And that's not good for us. It's not the way we were intended to live. We're just not wired for that kind of stress.

Ever wonder why you feel so exhausted after a period of worry? Ever wonder why fear just seems to drain you? I think you would be hard pressed to find anyone who would legitimately disagree with the fact that fear and worry can and will do immense damage to your body and mind over time.

The longer I live, the more I'm convinced that we are fashioned for faith, not for fear and worry. To live in fear is to live against the reality of our creation.

The Problem

"And why do you worry about clothes? Look at how the lilies of the field grow. They don't work or make clothes for themselves. But I tell you that not even Solomon with his riches was not dressed as

beautifully as one of these flowers. God clothes the grass in the field, which is alive today but tomorrow is thrown into the fire. So you can be even more sure that God will clothe you. Don't have so little faith!"
(vv. 28–30)

Here, once again, Jesus puts his finger on the problem. He shows the basic reason our fears get the best of us.

We don't really have a fear problem.

We have a faith problem.

We've lost confidence that our heavenly Father will take care of us.

You see, fear, in and of itself, is really not a problem. As we've seen, simple fear is unavoidable. It's even necessary. But fear without faith is a big problem. Fear without faith will eat you alive.

I've noticed that even those of us who have trusted our heavenly Father with our eternities often have a tough time trusting him with our tomorrows. In fact, as far as I can tell, most of us Christians have the same basic worries as our non-Christian neighbors. Like everyone else, we worry about things like the economy, our health, our kids, our relationships. Like everyone else, we fear losing our jobs, getting sick, losing our houses.

Fear, in and of itself, is really not a problem.
But fear without faith is a big problem.
Fear without faith will eat you alive.

But we shouldn't be like everyone else! Our response to the threats we encounter should be so out of the ordinary that people are amazed. Not that we're not concerned, not even that we're not fearful, but we should react differently to threats from the world because our hope is anchored elsewhere.

The Answer to Fear

And that, I believe, is the answer to paralyzing fear, the antidote for fear of the unknown, the alternative to energy-sapping worry. Jesus spells it out in Matthew 6:33. If you want to begin retraining your mind, you have to live out this verse: "But seek first his kingdom and his righteousness, and all these things will be given to you as well" (NIV). At this point Jesus isn't just inviting us simply to change our perspective. He's inviting us into a entirely different way of thinking and living. He wants us to make his agenda for the world—his "kingdom"—our first priority.

Even in the midst of my crisis? Yes, especially in the midst of your crisis. Because your crisis will become less of a crisis when you replace your fear of the unknown with a healthy fear of God.

The Bible actually talks a lot about the fear of God. Proverbs 1:7, for instance, tells us that "the fear of the LORD is the beginning of knowledge" (NIV). But we're talking about a completely different kind of fear in such verses. We're not talking about a threat to our well-being. We're just talking about a healthy respect for God and his ways.

Throughout history, this kind of fear has given individuals courage, direction, and motivation to make tough choices and live in a God-honoring way. Oswald Chambers described this succinctly in *The Pilgrim's Song Book*: "The remarkable thing about fearing God is that when you fear God you fear nothing else, whereas if you do not fear God you fear everything else."[4]

Jesus is saying essentially the same thing in the Sermon on the Mount. He's saying, "If you want to get serious about doing battle with the fears that limit you, if you want to get serious about addressing the issues in your life that lead to chronic worry and anxiety, you've got to make a decision to put me and my agenda first."

In other words, you will fear it until you surrender it!

This, then, is the secret of retraining our minds to put fear in its proper place, break free of the worry habit, and avoid the paralysis of Plan B—even if we can't avoid Plan B altogether. It's a matter of focusing on what is most important, putting first things first, which, of course, is God's kingdom—his priorities, his plans, his agenda.

God's kingdom first . . . financial concerns second.

God's kingdom first . . . kids' problems second.

God's kingdom first . . . marital conflicts second.

God's kingdom first . . . singleness issues second.

His kingdom first . . . our wills, our concerns, our plans, desires, and dreams . . . second.

Putting it all, including our fear of the unknown, in the hands of the One who knows everything. And then moving forward because we can trust him.

Even in the dark.

SIX WHIPLASH

Have you ever had a hard time enjoying a certain season of life because you're afraid the bottom might fall out? I often hear people say things like "Sure, things are going fine, but who knows what's next?" Or they'll say, "I feel like I'm walking around just waiting for the next bomb to go off."

The truth is, in this world there is good news and there is bad news, and often one comes right behind the other.

I'll never forget sitting on the front porch at the house of my friends Rob and Rhoda Brock. We've done ministry together for years and know each other extremely well. I don't know if I've ever seen a couple give of their resources to help other people the way those two have. They're the kind of couple every church planter dreams of having on their core team—multitalented, generous, and committed to honoring and proclaiming God. They're also great parents. But neither of their two children have taken the path they would've hoped.

I still remember the day their son, Matt, came to me to tell me he had gotten a girl pregnant. She wasn't even a girlfriend. They just had a one-night, experimental-type encounter that turned out to have a lifelong impact. Rob and Rhoda were devastated. How could this happen to their straight-A, never-in-trouble, leader-in-the-youth-group son?

But it had.

Maybe the one thing more painful than not seeing our personal dreams come true is to watch the dreams you have for your children fall apart. The next several weeks and months were full of painful growth for the Brocks. While it took a lot of tears, prayers, and long conversations, God worked in their hearts. With a tremendous amount of grace they reached out to their son and the girl involved. Eventually they became incredible grandparents to Matt's beautiful baby.

Things looked good. People pointed to them as an example of a couple who had allowed God to take something that could be considered bad news and turn it into good news. Even when their dreams for their son shattered, they hadn't given up on God.

Then some seven years later their daughter, a senior in high school, got pregnant out of wedlock. And I thought, *Are you kidding me?* They probably thought it too. Could they endure such an emotionally draining situation again?

Sometimes it feels like life is full of these emotional whiplash moments where you're thrust from the peaceful and serene to the stressful and turbulent without a moment's notice—and sometimes again and again.

Good News/Bad News

I want to introduce you to a guy out of the Bible whose entire life was one good news/bad news story. In a way, he was the poster child for whiplash. Yet despite all the ups and downs of his life—or maybe because of them—we can learn some invaluable lessons from him.

When we're first introduced to Joseph in Genesis 37, we're told that he's his dad's favorite son. I guess that is kind of a good thing, but it makes his brothers extremely jealous. In fact, they hate him, which is a bad thing.

As Joseph continues living his young life as the "favorite," his dad decides to give him this beautiful coat. Beautiful coats as gifts would fall into which category? That's right—good news. Except the gift makes Joseph's brothers even more jealous, so they decide he has to die. They rip the coat off, beat him up, and throw him into a pit, planning to kill him later. This obviously would be considered a bad day—definitely bad news for Joseph.

However, one of his brothers feels sorry for him and decides they probably shouldn't kill him, which is good news if you like breathing. But instead of welcoming Joseph back into the family, the brothers decide to sell him into slavery.

And you thought your family was messed up! I have a younger sister, and I'll admit that I thought about selling her a few times, but I never actually followed through with it. Unbelievably, these guys do just that. They sell Joseph to a caravan of merchants, who take him far away to the land of Egypt.

When he gets to Egypt, the good news is that Joseph gets a job with Potiphar, a head-honcho Egyptian dude. Joseph's a hardworking guy, and the Scripture also tells us that he's good looking (kind of like singer Keith Urban, whom my wife thinks is incredibly good-looking, though I'm actually one inch taller than he is . . . but I digress). This is all good news for Joseph, and he must be thinking that life is looking up.

Unfortunately, Potiphar's wife decides she's attracted to Joseph and tries to seduce him. Joseph resists her, but because he just needs some more bad news, she makes up a story, and he's thrown into prison.

But the story doesn't end here. While in prison, which is a lot like the pit he was in when this whole story began, Joseph forms a relationship with a guy who has the power to get him out. He does this guy a favor, and the guy promises to get Joseph released from prison.

Good news, right? Except the guy forgets Joseph, so Joseph has to spend two more years in prison, which is very, very bad.

Joseph's story almost seems unbelievable. But then again you've probably been there. Maybe not quite so many times as Joseph, but you recognize that whiplash feeling. You've been in the good-news season of life where you feel things couldn't get much better, only to transition into a crushing, bad-news period.

Maybe you prayed for a particular job and were thrilled when you finally got it . . . only to find out your boss was a total jerk who made your life miserable.

Maybe you remember celebrating the fact that you finally got pregnant after years of trying and praying . . . only to miscarry a few weeks later.

Maybe you stood there at the altar gazing into the eyes of someone you thought you would be with for the rest of your life . . . but something happened. Now you're staring into the same person's eyes across a courtroom.

What do you think our response is to be when we go from the good-news part of life into the bad-news season where everything seems to be falling apart, from our desired Plan A into a Plan B we never asked for and don't want? I think there is a question that can lead us into a deeper, more intimate relationship with God . . . if we have the guts to ask it.

The question is this: What would you do if you were absolutely confident God was with you?

When you respond in your current circumstances as if you were confident that God is there, you will see God in the circumstances.

Say your marriage is unraveling and you're hitting the panic button. What would you do if you were confident God was with you?

Or what if your kids are running from God and you're losing sleep each night worrying about them? What would you do if you were confident God was with you?

Or suppose you go to the doctor to check out a few annoying symptoms, only to find out you have multiple sclerosis. What would you do if you were confident God was with you?

The point? Simply this: When you respond in your current circumstances as if you were confident that God is there, you will see God in the circumstances. Maybe not immediately but eventually.

Because the simple truth is that God *is* there. God is always there. The problem comes when we allow our circumstances to distort our perspective and we miss God.[1]

Questions

That happens so easily when we're reeling from bad news in our lives. There's nothing like the whiplash of a painful situation to leave us feeling that God is a million miles away.

I bet this was how David felt when he wrote this psalm:

> *I thirst for the living God.*
> *When can I go to meet with him?*
> *Day and night, my tears have been my food.*
> *People are always saying,*
> *"Where is your God?"*
> *When I remember these things,*
> *I speak with a broken heart.*
> *I used to walk with the crowd*
> *and lead them to God's Temple*
> *with songs of praise.* (Ps. 42:2–4)

And imagine how Joseph must have felt sitting in the bottom of the pit. Can you imagine the pain of rejection he felt as a result of the violent and vicious act committed against him by his own brothers? He couldn't help it that his brothers were so jealous of him. Well, maybe he was a little spoiled. But still, he didn't deserve this!

He had to be lonely, scared, and full of questions: *I mean, if God really cared about me, would I be here right now?* He had to be banging his head up against the side of the pit, moaning, "Why me? Why me? Why me?"

You've been there, right? Not necessarily in the bottom of a pit, but you know that "why me" feeling. You've been lying in bed late at night, staring at the ceiling, unable to sleep and silently praying, *Why? Why me, God? Why now?*

You may also have been in that lonely place where you've screamed, "God, where are you? Why aren't you listening? Why have you abandoned me?"

When life isn't turning out the way we had hoped, we almost always default to feeling as if God has abandoned us.

We may not like to admit that. It makes us feel petty and immature. But it's the truth, isn't it? Don't we tend to wrap our own plans, our dreams, and our desires around our concept of God's presence so that when our plans and dreams and desires are frustrated we assume that God is just not there anymore? When our plans, dreams, and desires crumble, our faith tends to take a hit. We instantly feel let down and distant from our heavenly Father.

And yet the truth is that God is most powerfully present even when he seems most apparently absent. He's always working. Even when we can't see him or feel him, all the circumstantial evidence of our lives will testify to his presence.

That is, if we're willing to pay attention.

When life isn't turning out the way we had hoped,
we almost always default to feeling as if
God has abandoned us.

On the Edge of the Water

You may be familiar with contemporary Christian music artist Tammy Trent. You even may have heard her story. If so, I hope you'll be patient because this is one tale worth telling again.

It began in September of 2001, when Tammy was invited on a mission trip to Jamaica. Her husband, Trent (she had taken his first name as her last name), was going along because they planned to take a week of vacation before the mission trip started. They had a fantastic week together in Jamaica. Then, with one day left before the mission trip, Trent decided he wanted to go diving in the blue lagoon, a famous water hole just east of Port Antonio. He had been a certified diver since age twelve, so Tammy wasn't worried. It was just a lovely last day in what had been a memorable vacation.

After driving out to the blue lagoon, Tammy and Trent had lunch beside the dock. They chatted while Trent put on his wetsuit and fins and then sat together for a while beside the deep blue water. Tammy even took a few pictures at Trent's request. Then Trent slipped into the water.

"Baby," he said, "I'll just be about fifteen minutes. When I get back, we'll go and do something that you want to do."

"Okay, Trent," she answered nonchalantly.

Tammy watched her husband slip into the water and swim out toward the deep hole he wanted to explore. About halfway there, he lifted his head out of the water, and he waved good-bye. Tammy waved back.

She had no idea it would be the last time she'd ever see Trent alive.

Trent was free-diving that afternoon—diving without an oxygen tank. So as Tammy sat there watching the water, she would see him bob up every few minutes and catch a breath. She finished her lunch. She got distracted by a boat and some snorkelers in the area.

Then suddenly she realized it had been more than thirty minutes since she last saw Trent come up for air.

It's okay, she told herself, trying not to panic. *Everything's fine. Trent's a great diver. He's made this kind of dive a million times. There's nothing to worry about.*

But Tammy was worried. In fact, she was frantic. The men in the boat took her out to search, but they couldn't find Trent. Divers were called in, but they had to give up when darkness fell. All Tammy could do was wait and pray—and prepare herself as best she could for what they would find.

They recovered Trent's body the next morning.

This was the single most terrifying event in Tammy's life, and she was in a location where she knew no one. Her family, her friends, and her church were thousands of miles away, trying to make arrangements to get to her. And Tammy was in shock, feeling hopeless and fearful and scared and numb. Knowing God was with her—she never really doubted that—yet feeling totally alone.

She was sitting in her hotel room, trying to get her head around what had happened, when another guest called to her to turn on the television. She switched it on just in time to see a jet plow into the twin towers of the World Trade Center.

That day was September 11, 2001.

Tammy just stood there in shock, thinking, *What does this mean? The world is falling apart. America is falling apart.* Nothing seemed to make sense. She just kept wondering, *What now? What now, God?*

But a couple of days later while Tammy's family and friends were trying frantically to get her home, Tammy had an experience she will never forget. She remembers sitting alone in her hotel bathroom, weeping and crying out to God. With tears racing down her face, she desperately prayed, "God, I need to know that you're real! Are you there? Can you hear me? Can you see me? Do you feel the pain that I feel?"

At that moment, she found herself longing desperately to be with someone who loved her. All American flights were grounded because of the 9/11 tragedy, so no one in the family could get to her. She missed her mother especially—and she told God so. She said, "God, if you can hear me, could you just send me somebody to hold me? I'm not asking for thousands of angels or even hundreds, just one angel who will hold me."

Silence. Tammy sat there a little while longer, sniffling. Then, somehow, she got the impression that she was supposed to get up and leave the bathroom. She walked into the adjoining room and was puttering around there when she heard someone moving around. She stuck her head out into the hall and noticed the door to the adjoining room was open. Inside she saw a beautiful Jamaican woman standing there in a Hilton hotel uniform.

Tammy looked at the women and asked, "Ma'am, could you come in and make my bed?"

The woman said yes. But she also said, "I've been trying to get to you. I could hear you crying, and I've been trying to get to you. Could I just come in and hold you?"

"It was an instant answer to my prayer," Tammy remembers. "Everything that I'd ever longed to experience before in my walk with God happened right there. I had asked, 'God, could you just show up here right at this moment?' And he did it for me at that moment. So I knew . . . that somehow I would get through this. I knew that God was very, very real . . . I knew I was not alone."[2]

Can you believe that story? It floored me when Tammy shared it with me, and it still floors me. I asked Tammy what she would say to other people who are going through a painful Plan B experience. After a long pause she said, "I would tell them to step back from the chaos. We can't see clearly when we're in the middle of it. Take a deep breath. Let the wind blow across your face. Whatever your challenge, you will get through this."

Because no matter how things look, God is with you.

With Me?

God doesn't always grant such dramatic answers to prayer, of course. He doesn't always grant such powerful proof that he's present and working in our lives in the midst of a Plan B. Most of the time the signs are more subtle. And sometimes, to be honest, we find it really hard to believe God is with us, especially when we're living in Plan B.

But let me show you something interesting in this story of Joseph. It might be a bit confusing at first, but bear with me:

> Now Joseph had been taken down to Egypt. Potiphar, an Egyptian who was one of Pharaoh's officials, the captain of the guard, bought him from the Ishmaelites who had taken him there. The LORD was with Joseph and he prospered, and he lived in the house of his Egyptian master. (Gen. 39:1–2 NIV)

Did you catch it? "The LORD was with Joseph." Isn't that interesting—or is it confusing and surprising?

"The LORD was with Joseph"?

This whole story could really mess with your theology if you let it. I mean, didn't Joseph just get beaten up by his own brothers? Didn't he just get captured and taken to a foreign land? Wasn't he a slave?

Growing up, I always assumed that "the Lord is with you" meant things were going great. It meant your parents weren't going to get a divorce. It meant you'd gotten into the college of your choice, married the guy or girl of your dreams, and bought the house you'd always wanted. If the Lord was with you, it meant you'd landed the corner office, right?

Well, it's true that Joseph was doing pretty well when we see him in this passage. But notice *why* he's doing well:

When his master saw that the LORD was with him and that the LORD gave him success in everything he did, Joseph found favor in his eyes and became his attendant. Potiphar put him in charge of his household, and he entrusted to his care everything he owned. From the time he put him in charge of his household and of all that he owned, the LORD blessed the household of the Egyptian because of Joseph. (vv. 3–5 NIV)

Do you see that? Joseph isn't confident that the Lord is with him because things are going great. It's the other way around. Things are going well for Joseph because he believes the Lord is with him. Apparently he's believed it all along. Even when he was in the pit. Even when he was lurching along on a merchant's camel. Even while living as a slave in someone's house.

Like Tammy, he probably had moments and even days when he just couldn't feel God's presence. But he trusts God is there. And it shows. The master notices something special about this kid—something that speaks of God's favor—so he promotes him.

I think this is really important to note. Joseph may have been stripped of his coat but not his identity. He may have been rejected and abandoned by his family, but he has never stopped depending on his God. And even though life is certainly not turning out the way he assumed it would, he's making a choice to respond in all circumstances as if God is with him.

He doesn't have to make that choice. He could complain and become bitter. He could say, "Screw this—I'm out of here. A week ago I owned slaves, and now I am one." But he doesn't. Instead he has enough faith to figure out maybe God has a plan in everything that has happened to him. *Maybe God could use me here. This certainly isn't in the plans I had for myself, but maybe God has a different set of plans.*

That brings us to the tricky question of God's will.

God's Will

The single most common question I get from people in church circles is, "How do I discover God's will for my life? How do I know what job I should take or what person I should marry? How do I know what God wants me to do with my life? How do I know I'm doing what God wants?"

When people ask me how they can know God's will for their lives, I tell them the best first step is to know God. Beyond that I really don't have any steps.

Questions like these seem even more difficult to answer when our plans have been diverted toward Plan B and we're having our doubts that God is anywhere nearby. Often people automatically assume if they're going through a Plan B crisis they must have misunderstood or reinterpreted God's will. A lot of them are intensely concerned about figuring out God's will so that things can get back to normal.

The trouble is, it's not that simple.

When people ask me how they can know God's will for their lives, I tell them the best first step is to know God. Beyond that, I really don't have any steps. You have to understand that knowing God's personal will for your life, knowing his specific will for your life, is not a science. There is no magical equation. It's often a matter of trial and error. Sometimes we get it all wrong. And sometimes we have no clue whether we're getting it right until much later.

Chapter 16 of the book of Acts contains an interesting story where Paul is preparing to travel to Asia because he feels he's supposed to go there and preach. He believes it's God's will. And if anyone knows God's will, it's Paul, right? He may be one of the most significant individuals to the Christian movement ever. Clearly he's walking with God and listening to God. But something is a little off with that because Acts 16:6 tells us that the Asia trip just isn't working out. The text actually says Paul is "kept by the Holy Spirit from preaching the word in the province of Asia" (NIV).

Did he get it wrong?

You may remember a time when you've run up against a roadblock like that.

You finally found the right person to marry, but the wedding had to be canceled.

You applied to graduate school, but were then unable to get a loan.

You were ready to go back to work, but you got pregnant again.

You invested the money responsibly; then the market crashed.

You were pretty sure you were going in the direction God was leading, but all of a sudden you're filled with doubt because things aren't turning out like you expected.

Now, when the Bible says the Holy Spirit won't let Paul into Asia, it's not clear what that means exactly. Is Paul physically stopped—perhaps by a storm or an accident? Does a trusted advisor argue about the venture? Does Paul just not have a sense of peace about his plans?

We just don't know. But we do know he ends up in a place called Troas. He has absolutely no idea what's next. And quite frankly this brings me a lot of comfort. I can't tell you how many times I've been at that point in my life. I thought I knew exactly what God's will was for me. But as I pursued that direction I ran into a wall, a Plan B situation, and I ended up in Troas wondering what in the heck was going on.

I think there are a lot of us in Troas, right? We're waiting around because we don't know what's next. But according to Erwin McManus, part of the problem is that we're asking the wrong questions.

Commenting on this very passage in Acts, McManus points out that Paul doesn't know the what, when, and where of his circumstances. He doesn't know exactly *what* he is supposed to be doing. He doesn't know *when* he will know—is it tomorrow or next year? And he doesn't know *where* he will go. He had assumed it was to Asia, and now he's in Troas. (Later in Acts 16, we learn that he is called to Macedonia.)

But if Paul doesn't know the what, when, and where, he does know the answer to one important question. He knows *why* he's doing what he's doing. He knows his purpose, his mission—to bring glory to God with his life.

I'm afraid that most of us tend to do the opposite, especially when our Plan B situations are unfolding.

We spend a lot of time worried about *what* is happening to us—

- Is this disease fatal?
- Will our kids turn out all right?
- Can we pay the gas bill?

We focus a lot of attention on *when* things might happen—

- How long will our savings hold out?
- When will the kids finally move out of the house?
- When will the adoption go through?
- How long before our credit is repaired?

And we ask a lot of questions about *where* we will end up—

- Where am I going to live?
- Where am I going to work?
- Is this where I'm supposed to be?

The problem is, most of us get so focused on the what, when, and where that we neglect the most important question, which is *why*.

Think about Joseph. I'm sure that all the way through his journey, throughout that whiplash-inducing series of Plan Bs (or should that be

Plans B?), he has to be trying to figure out what God's will for his life is. But I think Joseph figures out early on that he had limited control over what, when, and where. Every time he gets close to figuring out what his next step will be, his life seems to take another drastic turn.

About the only thing Joseph can control about his life, in fact, is why he does what he does. He can live intentionally, choosing to trust God in all his circumstances and allow his life to be used for God's purposes.

Often in life, the what, when, and where are not going to turn out the way you want them to turn out. You don't always get to choose those things, but you do get to choose the why.

You may not get to choose where you work, but you do get to choose why you work.

You may not get to choose when you become a parent, but you do get to choose why you want children.

You may not get to choose what your future is going to be, but at any given time you do get to choose why you're living the way you do.

If you can focus on the why, the what, the when, and the where will come. Hang on to your central purpose, and one way or another, the other details will work themselves out.

Process Matters

Our focus on the what, when, and where in our Plan B situations proves we often misunderstand something important about God's will—which is that it's often a process, not a final destination.

Here's something else we often misunderstand about God's will: it's as much about the person we're becoming as it is about where we're going.

Here's an example. You feel led to try for a job. You go through the interview process, but you don't get hired. And you may assume, *Oh, I missed it. I guess it wasn't God's will for me to interview.* But maybe that's not the case at all. Maybe God wanted you to learn something through that process of interviewing. Maybe you just thought you missed God's will because you focused on the endpoint instead of on the process.

Just because God calls you to some venture, that doesn't guarantee the venture will succeed. Just because life doesn't turn out the way you thought, that doesn't mean you missed God's will.

And here's something else we often misunderstand about God's will: it's as much about the person we're becoming as it is about where we're going.

Almost eight years ago I made the decision to move back to my hometown of Nashville. That meant leaving the church I had started in Kentucky five years earlier—a church I absolutely loved. I just felt God prompting me to get out of my comfort zone again.

So I came to work at a church here in Nashville, and on my first day on the job I knew it was not a good fit. I remember putting my head on the desk and thinking, *Pete, what have you done?*

For the next several months I really struggled in that situation. I found myself praying over and over, "God, I thought this was your will. God, I thought this is what you wanted me to do. How did I miss this? How did I screw this up?"

I think it was Pastor Rick Warren who said, "God is more interested in your character than your comfort."[3] During the year I would spend at that church, I would discover how true that really is. The thing is, God had a few things he wanted me to learn. He wanted to refine and renew and recalibrate a few aspects of my heart and soul and, yes, my character. What he did in my life over that period of time has been invaluable in my last six years of life and leadership.

I think that might be helpful for you to keep in mind during those

Plan B moments when you're confused and frustrated about what seems to be happening in your life, when the plans you thought were from God just aren't working out. But is it possible God is trying to do something with who you are?

Maybe he called you to love the person who broke your heart because he wants to soften your heart.

Maybe he called you to interview for the job because he wants to teach you obedience and perseverance.

Maybe he put you in a city you can't stand, a city where you're totally out of place, because he wants to increase your reliance on him.

I love what Erwin McManus said about this: "The process of becoming the person God wants us to become usually doesn't come from success, success, success. It's loss, success, failure, success, heartbreak, success, disappointment, success."[4]

This reminds me of what C. S. Lewis wrote in his novel *The Great Divorce*. In it the writer, George MacDonald (a real man but also a character in the book), says,

> Ah, the Saved . . . what happens to them is best described as the opposite of a mirage. What seemed, when they entered it, to be the vale of misery turns out, when they look back, to have been a well; and where present experience saw only salt deserts memory truthfully records that the pools were full of water.[5]

In other words, our view of what God wants and what he is doing in our lives is way too limited.

We tend to think God is with us only when everything is working great and all the charts of our life are going up and to the right. We think that our Plan B situations are signs that we're not where God wants us to be. We think our suffering is a sign that we're getting something wrong, not evidence that God is at work to teach us and bring us blessing.

Choosing Whom

This brings us back to Joseph, who somehow got it right. Because with crisis after whiplash-inducing crisis, Joseph was making a very important decision that kept him from being caught up in a cycle of disappointment and bitterness. He was choosing why instead of getting hung up on what, where, and when.

More important, he was choosing *whom* he was going to trust. He chose to believe in God instead of his current circumstances.

Every one of us must make a very important decision and this decision will have huge implications on how we process life. We must decide if we are going to put our faith in what God does or in who God is.

In this life, many of your questions will simply not have answers. But through it all, God himself will never change. This is why our faith must rest on his identity and not necessarily his activity.

If you place your faith in what God does, you'd better prepare yourself for frustration and disappointment because you're never going to figure out God's ways this side of heaven. That's because God is God! As he told the prophet Isaiah . . .

> *Just as the heavens are higher than the earth,*
> *so are my ways higher than your ways*
> *and my thoughts higher than your thoughts.* (Isa. 55:9)

Why are you going through what you're going through? I don't know.

Is what you're doing God's will for your life? I don't know.

Will it be over soon? I don't know.

You may not know either. You may never know. In this life, many of your questions will simply not have answers. But through it all, God himself will never change. This is why our faith must rest on his identity and not necessarily his activity.

And who is he?

He is the God who is faithful. The God who keeps his promises. The God who is with us every moment and is in the process of working all things for good. Even in our whiplash moments. Even when the bottom seems to be falling out and bad news sets our heads to spinning.

Even in the midst of a Plan B, you really have only one task, one calling.

And that is to do what you would do if you were confident God was with you.

SEVEN WHAT HAVE YOU DONE FOR ME LATELY?

The other day I was catching up on some e-mails at home. It was a Saturday morning, and my kids were in the middle of their Saturday morning cartoons ritual. As a side note, I want to clearly state that I don't think cartoons are as good today as they were twenty-five years ago. Not even close. Then again, how do you compete with Smurfs and the Snorks?

Anyway, the TV was too loud, and our remote is currently broken. (Our new puppy somehow mistook it for one of his chew toys.) So I asked our eight-year-old, Jett, if he would get up and turn the TV down. He looked at me and asked, "Dad, what have you done for me lately?"

I thought, *Whaaaat?* (Okay, I actually thought something else, but this is a Christian book.) *What have I done for you lately? You mean besides providing your food, your clothing, and the roof over your head? Besides raising you, buying gifts for you, and unconditionally loving you?*

My ungrateful, cartoon-watching son was reflecting to me a very prevalent attitude among those of us who call ourselves Christ followers. Isn't it true you find it more difficult to be obedient and faithful when you feel as if God isn't doing anything for you? Don't you find yourself questioning God when he doesn't show up for you in the way you thought he was going to show up?

I think we often treat God like we do a vending machine. When you walk up to a vending machine, you expect to insert the appropriate amount of money, press the correct number or code, and out will pop whatever you were hungry for. The whole process takes about forty-five seconds.

We're looking for a quick spiritual transaction that doesn't necessarily lead to a deeper level of intimacy but gives us what we want.

We expect the same thing with God. Maybe not consciously. Maybe we'd never say it. But we still assume that if we do all the right things, say all the right things, and have the right attitude, we can simply press a magic spiritual button and get whatever it is we desire in the moment. We're looking for a quick spiritual transaction that doesn't necessarily lead to a deeper level of intimacy but gives us what we want. And like children, we want it *now*!

The Mirror of Our Need

By far the most difficult season of parenthood I've experienced to date has been the first three or four months of each one of our boys' lives. The lack of sleep and constant crying were enough to push me over the edge, and to this day I still don't know how my wife survived it.

I can remember each one of our boys crying the moment he felt a tinge of hunger. Our babies were incapable of seeing us as anything other than people who responded to their needs. They weren't concerned about how tired we were or how stressed out we might have been. They never woke up at two in the morning and thought, *You* know, I'm a little hungry, but I know Mom and Dad must be really worn out, so I'm just going to go back to sleep and wait until around six or so. No, they screamed, they kicked, and they demanded we be there to take care of that tinge of hunger.

Our tiny babies always saw us in the mirror of their own need.[1] And that's exactly what we do with God. We start to see him in the mirror of our own needs. And when we do that, we rob him of his glory and wonder. Or rather, we rob ourselves of the God we *really* need—the God who isn't at our beck and call, who isn't merely a projection of ourselves.

A. W. Tozer's book *The Pursuit of God* changed my life in so many ways. I love this passage from Tozer because it points to the subtle temptation that is common to so many of us—worshiping our own desires rather than God.

Before the Lord God made man upon the earth He first prepared for him by creating a world of useful and pleasant things for his sustenance and delight . . . They were made for man's uses, but they were meant always to be external to the man and subservient to him. In the deep heart of the man was a shrine where none but God was worthy to come. Within him was God; without, a thousand gifts which God had showered upon him.

But sin has introduced complication and has made those very gifts of God a potential source of ruin to the soul.

Our woes began when God was forced out of His central shrine and "things" were allowed to enter. Within the human heart "things" have taken over. Men have now by nature no peace within their hearts, for God is crowned there no longer, but here in the moral dusk stubborn and aggressive usurpers fight among themselves for first place on the throne.

This is not a mere metaphor, but an accurate analysis of our real spiritual trouble. There is within the human heart a tough fibrous root of fallen life whose nature is to possess, always to possess. It covets "things" with a deep and fierce passion. The pronouns "my" and "mine" look innocent enough in print, but their constant and universal use is significant . . . They are verbal symptoms of our deep disease. The roots of our hearts have grown down into things, and we dare not pull up one rootlet lest we die. Things have become necessary to us, a development never originally intended. God's gifts now take the place of God, and the whole course of nature is upset by the monstrous substitution.[2]

Let's be honest. Isn't Tozer's description accurate?

Whenever we don't get what we asked for, don't we get upset? Don't we feel either that we've done something wrong that's keeping us from God's blessing or that something is wrong with God? Not getting what we want tends to rattle our faith.

It works the other way too. Whenever we are faithful, whenever we're obedient, whenever we do the right thing, at some level don't we expect that life is going to turn around for us?

- Our kids will turn around.
- Our bank account will be replenished.
- Our relationships will get easier.
- We'll climb the ladder faster.
- We'll feel better about ourselves.

I think most Christians fall into that fallacy at one time or another, living as though we have an unspoken agreement with God: "If I live a somewhat moral life, you need to keep up your end of the bargain by blessing my life and not allowing anything seriously bad to happen to me or my family."

At some level, we persist in thinking that if we do what we think God wants, we're entitled to a good life.

The only problem is, life just doesn't work that way. It doesn't now, and it didn't work that way in biblical times either.

It certainly didn't work out that way for Joseph.

Are You Kidding Me?

Remember Joseph, whose story we looked at in the last chapter? His life, remember, was a head-turning series of reversals, from good news to bad news to good and then back again. The last we heard, he was a slave in Egypt but had been promoted to the head of his master's household. But look what happened next.

> So Potiphar left Joseph in charge of everything he owned and was not concerned about anything except the food he ate. Now Joseph was well built and handsome. After some time the wife of Joseph's master began to desire Joseph, and one day she said to him, "Have sexual relations with me." But Joseph refused and said to her, "My master trusts me with everything in his house. He has put me in charge of everything he owns. There is no one in his house greater than I. He has not kept anything from me except you, because you are his wife. How can I do such an evil thing? It is a sin against God." The woman talked to Joseph every day, but he refused to have sexual relations with her or even spend time with her. (Gen. 39:6–10)

Can you imagine what a huge temptation that must have been for Joseph?

I've been trying to eat healthier lately. My big vices are French fries and pizza. My wife, Brandi, knows this and would never purposely try to tempt me. But just the other day she made French fries for the boys because they love them as much as I do. I walked by the stove to see the hot, salty, delicious-looking fries. Normally I could resist, but I was so hungry. Just one fry, right? Maybe a handful? If I waited just a few minutes, I could have my appetite completely filled with the dinner Brandi had prepared for us. But in that weak moment I caved. I ate almost every one of those fries.

I've found it's much easier to fall into temptation when our needs are not being met. When we feel as if God has abandoned us, why not just go ahead and abandon him? Not having our dreams and desires fulfilled leaves us hungry, and when we're hungry we're tempted to fill that hunger with something that isn't good for us.

And you've got to assume that Joseph is hungry. He's a slave, after all. He's far away from anyone who cares for him. He's probably frustrated and lonely. It would be so easy for him to think, *I know this is wrong, but what the heck? Maybe this is my way out. Maybe this could be an escape from the pain I'm feeling. Nothing else is going right, so why not?*

Not having our dreams and desires fulfilled leaves us hungry, and when we're hungry we're tempted to fill that hunger with something that isn't good for us.

But look at what happens. Potiphar's wife just keeps on coming after him, begging him to sleep with her, and Joseph manages to resist.

You might read about this dramatic situation and think, *Oh man, what character. What strength. If ever God is going to reward faithfulness in the midst of a shattered dream it's going to be now.*

Right? Hmm. Read on:

One day Joseph went into the house to do his work as usual and was the only man in the house at that time. His master's wife grabbed his coat and said to him, "Come and have sexual relations with me." But Joseph left his coat in her hand and ran out of the house. When she saw that Joseph had left his coat in her hands and had run outside, she called to the servants in her house and said, "Look! This Hebrew slave was brought here to shame us. He came in and tried to have sexual relations with me, but I screamed." (vv. 11–14)

Holy Moses! Are you kidding me? This has to be a horrible joke. Surely this isn't happening to Joseph. After everything he's been through, it just can't. But it is.

Now, let me show you one more thing that may really confuse you.

So Potiphar arrested Joseph and put him into the prison where the king's prisoners were put. And Joseph stayed there in the prison. But the LORD was with Joseph. (vv. 20–21)

There it is again. Joseph's now been rejected, beat up, sold into slavery, falsely accused of rape, and thrown into prison. He's done the right thing in an excruciatingly difficult situation, and he's been punished for it. He's living out that painful cliché that no good deed ever goes unpunished.

But the Scripture keeps insisting that the Lord was with him.

How can that be?

But that's exactly what a lot of us feel in our Plan B situations— like we've done all the right things but still we're being punished:

- You've been a faithful husband, and still she cheated.
- You've served the company for years, and it laid you off.
- You tried to help someone, and she sued you.
- You tried to be honest with a friend, and he retaliated.

Then we sometimes see other people doing the wrong thing, and they get away with it. It is one thing to go through a Plan B because you did something wrong. It's something else entirely to do your very best, do nothing wrong, and *still* have your plans crash down around you. It's just not fair!

So . . . is God still with you even when that happens?

I believe the answer is yes . . . but that might not mean what you want it to mean.

Just One Thing

Joseph's story continues. Joseph makes a couple of friends in prison. There's a butler and a baker. Both his friends have dreams and ask him to interpret their dreams. Well, according to Joseph, the butler's dream means great news—he is going to be set free. This is great news for Joseph too. He's been sitting in prison waiting for just a time like this. He tells the butler:

> "When you are free, remember me. Be kind to me, and tell the king about me so I can get out of this prison. I was taken by force from the land of the Hebrews, and I have done nothing here to deserve being put in prison." (Gen. 40:14–15)

Joseph is making a very reasonable request, a simple favor. Remember me. When you're set free, remember me.

The butler seems to be agreeable to the plan and is eager to help Joseph out. And three days later, just as Joseph predicted, the butler is let out of prison. But then we read these disappointing words: "The officer who served wine did not remember Joseph. He forgot all about him" (v. 23).

Can you imagine Joseph's conversation with God when that happened? "God, after all this. I've been so faithful. All I asked for was this one thing. Just let the guy remember me. Is that too much to ask?"

How many times have you said to God, "Just do this one thing"? How many times have you dropped to your knees and, through tears, begged God for just this one thing?

- Just turn my wayward kids around.
- Just get me this job.
- Just let my husband go to counseling with me.
- Just shift our circumstances this one time.
- God, I just need this one break.

How many times have you asked it . . . and the answer was not what you hoped for? How many times have you begged for things to get better . . . and they just got worse?

What about times like those? Is God still with you then? In such moments you're haunted by the thought, *God could have done something and yet he did nothing.*

All Alone

It's so important that you get this, and here's why. If it hasn't already happened to you it will happen. You are going to feel like you're pouring your heart out to God and your prayers are bouncing right back and nothing is changing in your circumstance.

You have been praying about a dream that feels like it's slipping; you've been praying about an unmet expectation. But nothing.

You pray, but you see no change in your circumstances.

You pray, but the thing you are dreading still happens.

You pray, but you still feel all alone.

And maybe not just alone. You feel like you've been kicked in the stomach. When the One you depend on to give you what you want doesn't do his job, you feel betrayed, let down, thoroughly disillusioned.

That's practically the definition of a Plan B circumstance. You could even say it's normal. Or at least it's not unusual.

Peter Scazzero describes it this way:

Our good feelings of God's presence evaporate. We feel the door of
heaven has been shut as we pray. Darkness, helplessness, weariness, a
sense of failure or defeat, bareness, emptiness, dryness, descend upon
us. The Christian disciplines that have served us up to this time "no
longer work." We can't see what God is doing and we see little visible
fruit in our lives.[3]

And yes, even when you're going through all that, God is still with
you. But don't think that means it takes away your pain, anger, disappointment, and loss in that moment. Don't think you won't feel
the sting of injustice.

It took me a long time to figure all this out, to understand that
even when God is with me, life is not always going to turn out the
way I hoped. I knew there would be disappointments and struggles.
But part of me still wanted to believe my faith could act like a king-
sized ibuprofen. I wanted to believe that as long as I knew God was
with me, the pain of those difficult moments would be eased.

I'm finally getting it through my head—it just doesn't work that way.

For Joseph in prison, the fact that God was with him certainly
did not mean his good deeds were rewarded—at least not yet. It
didn't mean his prayers were answered—at least not for a long
time. And it certainly didn't make his loss hurt any less. He still
had to live there in prison, feeling forgotten and abandoned. He
still had to cope with the bad food and the hard stone floors and
the other prisoners. He still had to feel homesick and wronged and
lonely and forgotten.

Yes, even though God was with him.

How Does It Help?

So if knowing God's there doesn't ease your pain or solve your
problems or answer your questions, how does it help you?

I think that's a valid question. And if you're still thinking in vending-machine mode, you may not like the answer. If you're thinking in that "God owes me" kind of way, you may be in for yet another disappointment. But if you're willing to change your thinking maybe this story will help a little.

I remember being a freshman in college and feeling very alone for the first time. For the first time in my life, there seemed to be more people I didn't know than I knew. On top of that I was suddenly without the presence of my parents.

I went to college driving a baby-blue Buick Skyhawk I had bought from my grandfather a few years earlier. That car was a real chick magnet. Okay, not really. Though I did meet Brandi while driving that piece of junk, and miraculously she still went out with me.

I remember the first time my car broke down while I was in college. I stood there on the side of the road just wondering, *What in the world do I do now? Do I call a tow truck? Do I call a mechanic?*

This was before everyone had cell phones, so I found myself walking to a gas station. I needed to find a phone. I needed to call my dad. I didn't really expect he would be able to fix my car, but I knew he would know what to do next.

Dad told me he would drive up right after work to take a look at the car. And instantly I felt better. I still had a broken-down car on the side of the road. I still didn't know how we were going to fix it. But just knowing Dad was aware of my circumstances was a huge relief.

God Knows

At the end of the day, I think that is what so many of us long for. We just want and need to know that God knows what's going on with us, that we haven't been forgotten or abandoned. Even if we don't know what the outcomes of our current circumstances will be, there is a tremendous peace and comfort that comes with that.

And God does know. Isaiah 53:3 describes God's Son as "a Man of sorrows and acquainted with grief" (NKJV). He knows what it's like to be sad and disappointed. He knows what it's like to mourn and grieve. And while he's never promised to take the pain away, he has promised to be right there with us in the midst of it. He grieves with us. He's sad with us. He cries with us. He *knows*.

So that's one way that God's presence can help you while you're living Plan B: you can know that no matter how bad things get, and no matter how you feel, you're not alone.

But it wasn't just knowing that God was in the loop that made me feel better about my situation with the car. It also helped to know that my dad was going to help me . . . and that he knew what he was doing.

I didn't know exactly how long it would take. Dad said he would come after work, but that was a fairly long drive, and I didn't know what traffic would be like. I didn't know what Dad would be doing in the meantime. But I knew my dad. I knew his character. I knew he was both willing to help and capable of doing what needed to be done. So I was able to relax and wait for him to show up.

I think Joseph has that same knowledge to comfort him while he's still hanging out in that Egyptian jail. He doesn't know how things are going to work out. He doesn't have any delusions that his good deeds will be rewarded—he's learned better than that. He has no idea how long it will take for God to work things out. I mean, he's already waited years and years, and he's still sitting in the jailhouse.

But Joseph knows his dad. He knows his character. And that brings Joseph not only comfort but hope.

Joseph has faith that God is with him, and I think Joseph has faith that God is going to work something out for him. Not because he deserves it and not necessarily the way he thinks it should happen but in the best way possible.

How do I know that for sure? I don't. There's no verse showing what Joseph is thinking while his rear end is parked in that jail. But I get a pretty good clue in what Joseph says at the very end of his story.

You see, it took some time, but everything eventually worked out for Joseph. In fact, it turned out great. But God's plans involved a lot more than getting Joseph out of slavery or getting him a cushy job or getting him out of jail for something he didn't do. It involved a lot more than what Joseph wanted or needed in any given moment.

The Rest of the Story

Here's a quick rundown of what happened. Eventually the Pharaoh's butler does remember Joseph—right after Pharaoh has a dream that needs interpreting. The butler recommends Joseph as a dream interpreter. Joseph is able to interpret the dream correctly (it concerned a coming famine) and gives some advice (to store up food for the famine), so he is eventually put in charge of following his own advice. That means he is the highest official in Egypt. And Joseph is right there in his official position when his very own brothers—the ones who had beaten him and sold him—come begging for food.

After messing with their heads a little (hey, he was entitled), Joseph forgives his brothers and has them bring the whole family to Egypt. (In the process, as we read later in the Bible, he manages to save his entire people from destruction, but that's another story.) And once they are all together again (Gen. 45:4–8), he sums up the whole good-news-bad-news story of his life by telling his brothers what he kept on believing for so many years: "You intended to harm me, but God intended it for good to accomplish what is now being done, the saving of many lives."

But get this (because it's important too).

None of this happened for Joseph because he was good. None of it happened because Joseph asked and God was obliged to answer. It happened because God knew what he was doing with Joseph's life even when Joseph didn't have a clue. In those times when everything seemed to be going wrong and he could see no end in sight for his troubles, Joseph managed to keep hanging on to that.

And that's something you can hold on to, too, when in those Plan B times you just can't see an end to all your troubles.

He knows what you're going through. He is right beside you, sharing your pain, even though he may not take it away. And he knows what he's doing with your life, even if you don't.

Will you pause for just a moment and allow that truth to sink in? Let it ease your mind and your heart. Let it bring you strength and courage and peace and comfort.

God is with you. Right now. Right this moment. No matter how you feel.

But in order for that to make a difference in your life, you might have to change your thinking. You might have to give up some of your expectations about what God owes you and how things are *supposed to be*.

What if we viewed our hardships and challenges as opportunities to be the men or women God has created us to be? What would happen if we stopped grabbing for what we're owed and tried to receive each moment with gratitude?

Receptive and Grateful

I was up really late last night reading Ronald Rolheiser's wonderful book, *The Shattered Lantern*. This sentence in particular captured my imagination: "The original sin of Adam and Eve, the prototype of all sin, is presented as a failure to be receptive and grateful."[4]

Just think about it for a second. God creates Adam and Eve and places them in the garden where they are surrounded by unmistakable beauty and all the goodness of life. They are experiencing the fullness of life, life the way it was intended to be, and they're promised it will continue under one condition—that they just don't eat the fruit of a certain tree.

So what do they do? You know the story. Instead of gratefully receiving life as the gift it is and following the conditions of its giving, they try to seize it as if it were owed to them.

When I think of the sin that creeps into my own life, it usually begins with this same failure to receive life as a gift. My lust, my pride, my anger, my lack of forgiveness—all that comes from a heart that believes I'm entitled to something.

I'm wondering how different life would be for each one of us if we chose to view our circumstances and our relationships as the gifts they are. What if we viewed our hardships and challenges as opportunities to be the men or women God has created us to be? What would happen if we stopped grabbing for what we're owed and tried to receive each moment with gratitude?

Yes, even the unfairness of our Plan B pain.

The thing is, God is God. He doesn't owe any of us anything.

But he gives us everything, including himself.

He does it in his own magnificent, mysterious, maddeningly unpredictable way. He does it in his own time, which sometimes takes way longer than we think it should. He does it with the big picture in mind, with little regard to the way we think it should go. And so often, instead of giving us what we think we deserve, instead of taking away our pain and frustration and confusion in our Plan Bs, he offers us the promise of his presence.

But this is not a consolation prize. It's exactly the gift you need for what you're going through in any given moment. If you can trust in that, if you can receive that, you'll be in a better position to see what God is going to do next.

But can you do it? Can you honestly believe that God is with you?

Maybe the more appropriate question is: Will you believe it?

"Every day we have this choice to make," says Andy Stanley. "Am I going to define God by interpreting my circumstances or am I going to simply trust that God is who he says he is?"[5]

The decision isn't easy, but it can make all the difference.

It's a choice you can make every day, no matter what is happening.

Instead of griping that God isn't living up to your expectations, that he isn't meeting your needs the way you think they should be met, that he isn't answering your prayers with a vending machine *whoosh* . . . you can make the choice to receive what he is offering you in this moment.

The comfort of realizing he knows what you're going through.

The hope of realizing he really does know what he's doing.

EIGHT DARKNESS

Two of my favorite people in the world are Jeff and Vicki Rogers. My wife, Brandi, and I set them up on their very first date while we were in college, and Jeff was in the first discipleship group I ever led. Jeff and Brandi also worked with me in a student ministry that I was leading at a local church while in college.

In 2001, about the same time I was getting ready to launch Cross Point Church in Nashville, Jeff and Vicki felt a prompting to go into full-time missions, so they joined the staff of GO ministries based out of Louisville. They yearned to go to the Dominican Republic to spread the message of hope to an impoverished people group. I wasn't really surprised by their calling or their obedience to go. They've always been the kind of couple who was totally open to going wherever God led.

For the next several years, Jeff and Vicki split their time between the United States and the Dominican Republic. But with every trip south, their hearts were broken more and more for the Dominican and Haitian people to whom God was allowing them to minister. Finally, they made the decision to serve in the Dominican Republic full time. In January 2005, they started to sell or give away almost all of their possessions here in the States to make the big move.

I can remember thinking, *Do you really want to do that? Do you really want to move over there permanently? Why don't you keep your current arrangement of just splitting your time? You can have the best of both worlds. You get to do missions, but you also get to come back here to spend significant time with family and friends.*

Wisely, Jeff and Vicki didn't listen to people like me but followed their hearts and God's prompting. They did move to the Dominican Republic to follow their dream. But they had barely gotten there when Vicki was surprised to discover she was pregnant. And that wasn't part of the plan. While they weren't opposed to having children, they had really wanted to get settled into their new ministry in the Dominican before they even thought of starting a family. But now they knew they would have to leave the Dominican temporarily and travel back to the States to have the baby.

So this was a bit of a Plan B situation for the Rogers. But no biggie. They decided to just stay flexible and roll with the punches. They settled in to try to get their ministry off the ground before the baby slowed them down.

Several months into the pregnancy, Vicki's Dominican doctor told her he heard two heartbeats. Vicki told him, "Of course you do. Mine and the baby's, right?"

He said, "No, I hear two babies."

Clearly, their Plan B had a second chapter. With twins on the way, they would have to leave the island earlier than expected. So in June 2005, they reluctantly returned to the States. The plan was to have their twins in a safe environment and quickly return to the Dominican Republic, where they had left their hearts.

But Jeff and Vicki's story is far from over. A few weeks after they got to the States, an ultrasound revealed a serious and possibly fatal complication. Their twins were monoamniotic, which means they shared a single amniotic sac and a single placenta. This rare condition meant the baby girls only had a 50 percent chance of surviving in the womb.

Jeff and Vicki left the doctor's office that day shell-shocked, but still hopeful. The goal was to get to thirty-two weeks and then try to deliver the girls. The longer they stayed in the womb and the bigger they got, the more likely it was they would not make it.

They didn't even make that goal. At week twenty-seven, further complications forced Vicki to be admitted to the hospital for around-the-clock monitoring. And two weeks later, alarming test results forced the doctors to go ahead and deliver Sophie and Renea. Each twin weighed just two pounds. If they had waited even one more day, the doctors said, at least one of the girls would have died.

The twins were rushed to the neonatal ICU where they would spend the next six weeks fighting for life. Meanwhile, Jeff and Vicki were fighting for answers to some very difficult questions.

"We were facing the death of expectations," Vicki told me later. "I had dreams of baby showers and shopping with friends. The dream of just holding my girls after they were born. The dream of coming home to a nursery that was prepared just for them. The dream of healthy children who weren't hooked up to machines. All of these expectations were dying."

Then one night during their eight-week hospital stay, doctors informed Jeff and Vicki that little Sophie had developed a brain bleed. It was quite possible she would not make it through the night.

In that moment, Jeff and Vicki weren't sure they would make it either.

Can You Handle It?

Like you, perhaps, I grew up in church. And my overall experience with that was actually quite positive. I'm not one who walks around bitter and carrying a lot of baggage from my early church experiences.

However, there were several times in my life when well-meaning people spoke what they thought were scriptural truths into my life.

But those "truths," which actually were not scriptural at all, just created layers of distortions about how I relate to God.

One particular phrase I seemed to hear over and over was this: "God will never give you more than you can handle."

It sounds so sweet and biblical, like something my grandmother would have done in needlepoint and hung on the wall in her house.

The problem is, nothing could be further from the truth.

Where in the world did we get such a whacked theology? Where's that verse in the Bible? Hallucinations 4:32 maybe?

Let's consider Jeff and Vicki. They've dedicated their lives to following Christ and making an impact around the world. They are willing to give up their secure lives here in the States to serve as missionaries, only to go through one unbelievable setback after another. Now they are sitting in a lonely, dark hospital room, watching their twin girls fight for their lives and being informed that one of them might not make it through the night.

I don't know about you, but that just doesn't sound right to me. That doesn't sound like something the average person can handle, even with God's presence.

Here's the truth—and this one is thoroughly biblical: throughout life you will face one situation after another that will be completely beyond what you can handle.

The apostle Paul certainly did. He writes in 2 Corinthians 12:7 of a situation he calls "a thorn in my flesh, a messenger of Satan" (NIV). We don't know exactly what it was—a physical handicap or medical condition or a hard-to-break habit? Paul doesn't tell us. But he does tell us he couldn't handle it. He had to turn it over to God:

> Three times I pleaded with the Lord to take it away from me. But he said to me, "My grace is sufficient for you, for my power is made perfect in weakness." Therefore I will boast all the more gladly about my weaknesses, so that Christ's power may rest on me. That is why, for Christ's

sake, I delight in weaknesses, in insults, in hardships, in persecutions, in difficulties. For when I am weak, then I am strong. (vv. 8–10 NIV)

The Bible is packed with stories like that. In fact, most of the stories we learned in Sunday school are about individuals who faced situations that were completely beyond what they could handle.

Here's the truth—and this one is thoroughly biblical: throughout life you will face one situation after another that will be completely beyond what you can handle.

Situations that forced them to make a choice—either abandon God or worship him in the midst of a Plan B.

The Wall

Take Abraham, for instance. In his long lifetime, he faced one Plan B after another.

The first is described in Genesis 12 when God calls Abraham to leave everything that is familiar to him. God asks him to leave his family, his wealth, and the safety of the known to go to some unnamed land. And Abraham does it. He chooses to worship God through his obedience even in the midst of the darkness.

God promises Abraham he'll be the father of a great nation. But then Abraham finds himself in the midst of another Plan B—a disappointing situation called infertility. Here God has birthed an amazing dream and desire in Abraham's heart, but this dream seems to be going nowhere. This Plan B leads to all kinds of marital tension for Abraham, but he chooses to worship God through his faith even in the midst of his frustration.

Eventually Abraham does have a son named Isaac, and you believe everyone is going to live happily ever after. Surely God wouldn't allow him to go through more after he's been through so much, right?

Well, if you've been reading this book, you know better than to answer that question. In fact, Abraham's about to face the most painful Plan B situation anyone can imagine. God's about to test his faith by asking him to do the unfathomable.

> Then God said, "Take your only son, Isaac, the son you love, and go to the land of Moriah. Kill him there and offer him as a whole burnt offering on one of the mountains I will tell you about." (Gen. 22:1–2)

Can you imagine what these instructions do to Abraham? God is asking him to sacrifice his only son, the son he waited so many years for, the son who is supposed to be the fulfillment of God's promise. This isn't anything he can easily handle. It's not something anyone can handle!

What is happening here is that he's hit what Janet Hagberg and Robert Guelich call "the wall." He's reached the limits of what he is capable of doing.[1]

For most of us, the wall appears when we encounter a Plan B that turns our world upside down. It could be a divorce, a betrayal, a job loss. It could involve a sudden death, a disillusioning church experience, or maybe a deep depression. Any of these can push a person against the wall.

Whatever happens, we find ourselves at the end of our ability to handle our lives. We probably also find ourselves questioning ourselves, God, the church. We discover for the first time that our faith does not appear to "work." We have more questions than answers. We don't know where God is, what he is doing, where he is going, how he is getting us there, or when this will be over. The very foundation of our faith feels like it is on the line.

The wall can be a very dark place—as Jeff and Vicki discovered.

Thank God, Sophie survived that difficult night in the hospital. But there would be so many more hurdles for both girls, hurdles that would test Jeff and Vicki's faith over and over and over.

Finally, after five blood transfusions, staph infections, and a myriad of other health issues, the twins were able to come home. They seemed to have finally bounced back from their rocky start. But just a few weeks later, when the girls were four months old, Jeff and Vicki got more painful news. Both Sophie and Renea were profoundly deaf. The condition was entirely unrelated to the girls' prematurity. It came from a rare gene Jeff and Vicki both carried.

Like Abraham, when that diagnosis came, they found themselves facing their very own wall.

Letting Go

But here's something interesting about what Abraham does when he faced his wall. I find it almost unreal that Abraham, with no argument, delay, or seeming resistance, heads up the mountain to fulfill God's request. He doesn't even seem angry or bitter. He has to be wondering what God is up to, but he doesn't argue. He just sets out to obey. And remember, he doesn't have any idea at this point what will eventually happen. He doesn't know that God will stop him before he sacrifices Isaac. He really thinks God is taking him up the mountain to kill his son—and he's willing to trust God anyway.

How is it that Abraham could be so trusting? There are several possible answers to that question. But I believe one of the most important is that Abraham had developed the practice of gratitude in his life.

We see in several places throughout his life that Abraham builds altars to mark a moment in time when God fulfills a promise. For instance, in Genesis 12:7, he builds an altar to mark his family's arrival in Canaan, the land that God promised to give him. He builds altars again in Genesis 12:8 and Genesis 13:18.

I have to believe these altars served as trigger points for faith throughout the rest of his life. They reminded him of all the times God showed up in the midst of the impossible. They were a reminder of all the times God fulfilled his promises.

Jeff Henderson, pastor of Buckhead Church in Atlanta, puts it this way: "Abraham finds a way to remember, 'God is with us.' If you don't have a systematic way of remembering God's faithfulness in the past, God will shrink in your heart."[2] In other words, if you don't remember God's past faithfulness, you're going to have a hard time trusting him when you're up against the wall.

Year after year, then, Abraham builds altars of gratitude to remind himself he can trust God in all of his wisdom. So when Abraham finds himself up against the wall, he has something to go on. He can say, this doesn't seem to make any sense. But the one thing I know is that I can trust the Creator of the universe.

So I've got to ask, what are some of your altars? What are the triggers that remind you of God's faithfulness throughout your life? Maybe it's a picture, a particular verse, a journal entry, or a child. Without these reminders, you will always be tempted to doubt, push back, or even walk away when you find yourself at the wall.

If you don't remember God's past faithfulness,
you're going to have a hard time trusting him
when you're up against the wall.

Stripped

After finding out their baby girls were deaf, Jeff and Vicki both slipped into a dark place. "We went home and just fell apart," Jeff told me.

"Surely, after all we've been through, God wouldn't allow us to go through something else. For months we had stood by their little units and sung songs, read Scripture, and whispered words of hope to our sweet girls, only to find out they couldn't hear a single word of it.

"We knew on that day that everything was going to be different," he remembers. "This is not the way we thought parenting was going to look. This is not the way we thought ministry was going to look. This is not the way we thought life was going to work."

I think this is a difficult truth to grasp, but God loves you enough to strip you of anything that keeps you from him. And often these things that separate you are not bad in and of themselves. Often, in fact, they're good things—relationships, missions, jobs. But if for some reason they are keeping us from knowing God as we should, he may take them out of our lives.

And that's what happens at the wall. That's why it's so painful—because we are being stripped bare. But that's what needs to happen because at the wall, there is a transformation from what we believe in our heads to a belief that permeates every fiber of our beings. More often than not, it involves a profound encounter with who we are and what we believe to be true in our core.

Hagberg and Guelich describe it this way: "The wall represents our will meeting God's will face to face . . . Fundamentally, it has to do with slowly breaking through the barriers we have built between our will and a newer awareness of God in our lives."[3]

Obviously, that's what was happening when Abraham hit his wall. His true heart, his allegiance to God, was being tested.

Jeff told me one day he felt like God had stripped him and Vicki of the Dominican Republic. He had been praying through all of this: "God, why? God, how could you? Is this the way you treat people who want to serve you?" And he felt as if God responded by saying, "Jeff, are you going to serve my kingdom the way I ask you to or the way you want to?"

It was in that moment Jeff realized, "The Dominican Republic had become an idol for us. It was an idol God was stripping away because it had become something we were using to compare ourselves to other people to feel better about what we were doing for God."

The wall is the place where I must relinquish what I cling to for identity! I must let go of that which holds me back from intimacy with God and worship of God. This could be work or religion or certain God-given gifts. It could be expectations or dreams, or it could be addictions. Maybe it's control or the desperate need for approval.

I don't know what it is for you. But I do know God is honored by faith and he will leverage anything in your life to expand and grow your faith.

Please understand, please prepare yourself because if you haven't come up against the wall yet, you will eventually. God will allow you to go through something. It might be a loss, a tragedy, a life-changing situation, and there will be no simple explanation to why it is happening.

Let's just be honest here. Time and time again in your life you're going to feel as if God isn't showing up. You're going to feel as if God isn't healing, he isn't restoring, he isn't releasing his mighty power.

These moments are crucial moments in your relationship with him. These moments are crucial because God is trying to get you to the place where you can't handle things on your own, where you are willing to surrender your plans in order to receive his. He's trying to mature your faith.

In moments like that, will you continue to choose to believe that he is who he says he is?

The Land of Uz

One of the best examples of someone hitting the wall would have to be found in the Old Testament story of Job.

We're told right off the bat Job is an "honest and innocent man"

(Job 1:1). He fears God and shuns evil. He is considered blessed because he has seven sons and three daughters and owns seven thousand sheep, three thousand camels, five hundred teams of oxen, and five hundred donkeys. I don't really have anything to compare this to, but it certainly sounds like a lot of stinking animals to me. I'm not sure I would call it a blessing to take care of that much livestock, but apparently in Job's day this was a sign of great wealth.

The story of Job takes place in the land of Uz—not to be confused with the land of Oz, where really short people, scarecrows, lions, and flying monkeys roam. Scholars believe the land of Uz was actually in a region of what we now know as Israel. This signifies that Job is not just the story of one man but actually the story of everybody—or, as I once heard it described, "the story of all of us."

The first thing we learn about Job, other than the fact that he's rich, is that Job is a good man, and good things are happening to him. It's almost as if he experiences good things in direct proportion to the amount of obedience he offers. And while most of us know deep down inside this isn't the way life always works, most of us still hold on to a thread of belief that this is the way life *should* work.

But the land of Uz is different. It's a place where very bad things can happen to very good people. John Ortberg describes it this way: "Uz will be a place, not just where suffering comes, but where it comes without warning and without explanation, creating confusion and despair."[4]

Uz, in other words, is a land of Plan Bs.

You may be familiar enough with the story of Job to know his first Plan B situation consists of losing his livestock, wealth, servants, children, and pretty much everything he cares about. Basically he's the subject of a bet between God and Satan, and what they're betting on is how he'll respond to losing everything.

And how does he respond? Initially, with an almost superhuman good attitude:

When Job heard this, he got up and tore his robe and shaved his head to show how sad he was. Then he bowed down to the ground to worship God. He said:

> *"I was naked when I was born,*
> *and I will be naked when I die.*
> *The LORD gave these things to me,*
> *and he has taken them away.*
> *Praise the name of the LORD."*

In all this Job did not sin or blame God. (Job 1:20–22)

Most of us can't even begin to comprehend responding to this level of suffering with worship and trusting words. Job's response is getting to the crux of what this entire story is really all about. Before all of this happened, Satan had made a key point. He said, "Job honors God for a good reason" (Job 1:9).

"People only love you because of what you give them," Satan's saying to God. "People will only follow you, they'll only commit to your ways, if there is an immediate benefit to them. Take away the blessings, take away the toys, take away those things, and you'll take away their devotion and their worship."

That's how the whole bet got started in the first place. It's about how far someone can be pushed before he will stop worshiping God.

Something's Not Right

So here comes the next devastating blow. Satan and God up the ante on the bet, and God allows Satan to afflict Job with these horrendous painful sores. As if it wasn't enough that all the things he cared about had been stripped from him, now he's in immense physical pain.

This time Job reacts a little differently. He doesn't sin, but he certainly starts to struggle. He starts to ask questions and slip into a season of discouragement.

This happens easily in the land of Uz, where it can get really dark. Sometimes this darkness can last for a long time. And with the darkness come unanswerable questions and the gnawing sense that things are not as they should be. The unanswerable question of why seems to make our suffering that much worse.

Have you ever wondered why it is we know things are not as they should be? How is it that we know there is right and wrong?

When Job lost his children and all of his possessions he knew something wasn't right.

When a plane flies into a building killing thousands, we know that's not right.

When you see children who grow up with no one to take care of them, we know that's not right.

When a four-year-old dies from a brain tumor or a mother of three dies slowly of breast cancer, we know that's not right.

When a woman is abused, we know that's not right.

When a missionary couple's babies are fighting for their lives and they can't return to the job they love because their children are deaf, we know that's not right.

Whether we believe in God or not, most of us know intuitively that there are certain things that shouldn't happen in the world. It's that intuition that makes us want to ask why in the first place.

But where does it come from? Why do we have this sense, not just that life is difficult, but that things are not the way they're supposed to be?

To answer this question, we have to take a quick detour back to the very beginning of the book of Genesis.

When God put Adam and Eve in the Garden everything in the world was the way it should be. Throughout the creation process the Creator said over and over: "It's good." The first man and the woman had everything they needed to be healthy and happy. And there was only one rule:

> The LORD God put the man in the garden of Eden to care for it and work it. The LORD God commanded him, "You may eat the fruit from any tree in the garden, but you must not eat the fruit from the tree which gives the knowledge of good and evil." (Gen. 2:15–17)

Did you notice what the forbidden fruit was? It was knowledge— the knowledge of good and evil. Once Adam and Eve disobeyed God and ate that fruit, they would know too much. They'd gain something they never had, something that would drive them crazy the rest of their lives. They would know when things are the way they should be and when things are all wrong.

That, of course, is exactly what happened. And because they had introduced sin into the world at the same time, they were now in a double bind. Because they ate the fruit, the "good" they now understood and yearned for would always be out of their reach. And also because they had eaten that fruit, they would have to live with that poignant and painful knowledge.

We, the descendants of Adam and Eve, have inherited this painful dilemma. No matter how hard we try, life will never be quite the way we think it should be. That's why we find it so disappointing that things aren't the way they're supposed to be. It's because there really is a way things are supposed to be—and according to the Bible it is stunning and splendid beyond our imagination.

The old Hebrew prophets used to dream about this "right way." They even had a word for it: *shalom.*

You may have heard the word used as a greeting, sort of like Hawaiians say aloha. But *shalom* is so much more than that. The word derives from *shalem,* meaning "whole, complete, perfect and

full." *Shalom*, in other words, means "all things the way they are supposed to be."[5] And one day, according to the Bible, they will be. But
not yet. Not while we're living in the land of Uz. While we're here,
we're going to keep running into situations that make us whimper
and wonder why—or shout the question in anger.

I don't know if you've ever thought about this, but only human
beings look for meaning in suffering. As much as Disney would like
for us to believe animals do this, they really don't. When you see a
cluster of buzzards on the side of a road, ripping into the carcass of
a dead deer, they're not pondering why this senseless act of violence
happened to one of God's creations. They're not circling around the
deer, crying out to God, "Why? Why did this happen to yet another
graceful deer?"

Only human beings have this longing for meaning in the midst
of incomprehensible, senseless pain. Only humans have this desire
to ask "Why? What's the purpose? Why does God allow it? Why is
everything all messed up?" And that desire, that need, only increases
the suffering we experience.

That may make it hard for us to even believe there is a God—or
that he cares about us. When we're living in the land of Uz, doubts
tend to come easily.

Doubting Believers

I received an e-mail the other day from a dear friend who happens to
be a very successful Christian musician here in Nashville.

I'm having a really hard time right now and need your prayers.
Over the last couple weeks I've become more and more sad to
the point now that I'm unable to enjoy myself at all. I'm hesitant
to call this depression because I don't know the real clinical def-
initions of that. It came and went at first—feelings of melancholy

to feelings of total despair and godlessness—but now it's all the time. (I am not suicidal.) On top of this, I'm having serious doubts.

First I had a hard time sleeping. I stayed up most of several nights in a row with intense feelings of worthlessness, small-ness, thinking about how short life is and how long eternity is, how large the universe is and how insignificant I am in it all, how meaningless it all is. Then I just grew more and more sad. No real reason at all. Life right now is actually as close to per-fect as it can be.

Then, I was doing research for a book I'm supposed to write about the kingdom of God and came across scholarly asser-tions that have caused me to doubt my belief in Jesus as the Son of God.

I can't defend against these accusations in this clouded state. And lots of other little nagging things bring doubt when-ever I read Scripture or try to find answers. I'm swallowed up in this, unable to laugh or even smile, unable to think straight. This e-mail is taking me forever to write.

I've read much more damning stuff against Christianity in the past and been unbothered by it. I know these assertions wouldn't bother me if I were in my right mind. But I'm not. I'm in a very dark place that has my brain spinning everything—every verse of Scripture—into doubt. It's as if the Spirit is gone and I can no longer see things through spiritual eyes—nothing resonates as true all of a sudden. All of this gradually over the last couple weeks.

I tell you all this—even though it's very, very embarrassing—because I need help. At the moment I believe in God and the power of prayer, and while that belief is here I'm asking you to pray. I don't know how you should pray, but please do.

I share this e-mail with you because what I know about this guy that you don't is that he has one of the purest hearts I know. He doesn't just want to make good music; he wants to make the world better. He yearns to help bring about the kingdom of God on this earth by living the most Christlike life he possibly can. He has an unwavering vision for the way this world should be.

Some people—usually called idealists or dreamers or visionaries—have a more acute sense of *shalom*. They feel the disconnect between what is and what should be more intensely than others. But most of us, deep down inside, have hidden hopes for a world much different from the one we must live in. Because we have these hopes, we're apt to get discouraged whenever we see how far from reality these hopes are.

And that, I believe, is where doubts set in for believers living in a Plan B world.

The French theologian Jacques Ellul had it just right: "The person who is plunged into doubt is not the unbeliever, but the person who has no other hope but hope."[6]

Actually, if you think about it, an unbeliever doesn't have to wrestle with doubt anyway. He can't really doubt something he doesn't believe in the first place. However, we believers can easily fall into doubt because even while we believe in God, we don't actually have proof. We're living "by what we believe, not by what we see" (2 Cor. 5:7).

Do you see what I'm saying? If you believe, if you have faith, then you will always be susceptible to doubt.

Stop believing, and you'll stop doubting.

Stop believing, and you won't see any need to question God.

Stop believing, and you won't be angry anymore—not at God, anyway.

Do you see what I mean? The more you believe in the possibilities of *shalom*, the more you long for the kingdom of God to be ushered into this hurting world, the more likely you are to fall into doubt from time to time, especially when you find yourself living a Plan B reality.

This is the inherent tension of the land of Uz. We're created for something so much more, so much better. But we currently find ourselves living in a broken world that's full of violence instead of peace, disease instead of health, and ultimately death instead of life.

No wonder we're plagued by doubts and questions.

No wonder we're angry.

No wonder we're haunted by why.

Anger and Confusion

We don't know how long the ordeal lasted, but it must have felt like forever. We do know that for a better part of the book (about twenty-eight chapters' worth) Job shoots his questions toward God. He never really reaches the point of doubt, but he expresses plenty of anger and confusion from his dark place.

And the whole situation is made worse by three friends who suggest to Job over and over that this calamity was brought on by his own sin.

Job's friends feel very familiar to me. Their arguments sound very much like the common religious misconceptions I grew up with. It was often impressed on me that people were not healed because they didn't pray enough or fast enough or read the Bible enough or even believe enough. If life wasn't working out and God wasn't showing up in the way you wanted God to show up, that meant you just weren't measuring up to what God wanted.

The real problem with this assumption, of course, is not just that it leads to out-of-control legalism. The real problem is not that it's supremely unhelpful. The real problem is that it's just not true.

And Job knows that. He knows his friends are completely wrong about him. Scazzero writes concerning Job, "He was an innocent sufferer. His friends had no room for the 'confusing in between,' no room for mystery. Like many Christians today, they overestimated their grasp of truth. They played God and stood in God's shoes."[7]

We're called to be faithful to God
even when it seems he hasn't been faithful to us.
We're called to love him
even when we feel abandoned. We're called to look for him
even in the midst of the darkness.
We're called to worship him even through our tears.

Sadly, I still see this happening today with a lot of people who are in the midst of a Plan B. They get stuck in the pervasive lie that says, "If you do good, God will bless you with good, and if you do bad, God will allow bad to happen to you."

Job knows better. So when his friends try to push this notion on him, he pushes back, insisting that his experience of suffering, pain, and loss is much more complicated than just a game of do bad, receive bad. But amazingly, while Job remains angry and confused through all this unexplainable tragedy, Job still manages to hang on to his faith. He questions God, he shouts at God, but he never really gives up on God. He stays engaged. Eventually, he lets God lead him into a stronger, better place, a place of wisdom and humility and deeper faith. And that's *before* God restores all his wealth.

Job is a reminder to all of us who live in the land of Uz. There will be times you seemingly will be doing everything right, and out of nowhere you'll be thrust into Plan B. Everyone experiences times of hurt and crisis, times when life turns out the way it shouldn't turn out, for we all live in the land of Uz.

Job is a reminder as well that we don't know how long we'll walk in the darkness. The deep hurt and the unanswerable questions could last another day or another four years, or it could quite possibly last a lifetime.

But Job is also a reminder that how we respond to God during these times really matters. We're called to be faithful to God even when it seems he hasn't been faithful to us. We're called to love him even when we feel abandoned. We're called to look for him even in the midst of the darkness.

We're called to worship him even through our tears.

Even in Uz

Recently I experienced a very moving moment in one of our worship services at Cross Point Church.

Earlier in the week, as I was preparing for a meeting with a few pastors who were in town, a woman came busting into our offices. I've known Jan for years and had never seen her like this. She was literally hysterical. My colleagues and I sat down with her, and I was finally able to begin to piece her story together through all the crying and weeping and uncontrollable shaking.

She had just found out that her husband of almost twenty years was having an affair. Her entire world was being turned upside down.

We were able to minister to both Jan and her husband that day, and then the rest of the week they spent some intense time with a wonderful Christian counselor. I heard that while the counseling had been going well, there was still no resolution to what was going to happen in their marriage. There was still too much pain, too many unanswered questions to know where they were going to go from here.

What makes their story so memorable to me is what I saw and experienced that very next Sunday, only four or five days after I had seen Jan and her husband in my office. I was standing in my usual spot down front during worship, and out of the corner of my eye a woman caught my attention. A second glance confirmed it was Jan with her hands raised, worshiping God with everything she had.

I remember getting very emotional in that moment. I remember thinking, *How is she able to worship in the midst of a crisis like this?*

But when I thought about it a little bit longer, I knew. It's because she was truly worshiping her creator. She wasn't worshiping her circumstances. She wasn't going through the motions. She was making a conscious decision to worship God even though internally I'm sure she was haunted by doubts.

She was choosing to worship as she made her journey down the middle of the land of Uz.

Nobody would have blamed my friend Jan if she was still at home curled up in a ball crying.

Nobody would have blamed her if she was yelling and cursing at God.

Nobody would have blamed her if she was so caught up in "Where are you?" and "How could you let this happen?" that she couldn't even darken the doors of the church.

But no, there she was, front row, arms held high, immersed in the worship of a God who circumstantially was nowhere to be found.

Light in the Darkness

Can you do that? Have you done that? When Plan B is creating havoc in your life and God doesn't seem to be doing a thing, can you still worship him? Can you still follow him? When he's not orchestrating the circumstances of your life in the way you desire, do you still trust enough to seek him with reckless abandon?

Abraham did that. Job did too, eventually. And so did Jeff and Vicki.

After the discovery of their girls' disability, they made a decision to stay here in the United States. Despite their deep longing to go back to the Dominican Republic, they finally decided God was telling them to stay home.

Vicki told me, "I think God broke our heart for the Dominican Republic so we could be better servants here in the U.S." Jeff and Vicki now are trying to use what God taught them in the Dominican Republic in all of the new mission fields he is providing right here at home. "We're sharing the love of Christ within the preemie community and the deaf community and in our neighborhood and anywhere God is allowing us to have influence and relationships."

It's amazing the bright light God allows our lives to become when we give him all we have in the midst of the darkness.

NINE ME TOO

Writer Anne Lamott has said that the most powerful sermon in the world consists of two words: *me too.*[1]

I believe she's on to something.

Because when you're struggling with a Plan B circumstance, when you are dealing with unmet expectations, when you're hurt or doubting, questioning and crying, there's nothing more healing than knowing someone else has been there. When you're hurt or doubting, there's nothing more comforting than hearing someone say, "I know what you're going through." When you're questioning and crying, there's nothing that helps more than being told, "I'm in it with you."

Me too.

When you're in a Plan B, you need community more than ever. And yet, because of the pain that comes along with a Plan B, it's easy to miss the God-given gift of community.

When other people draw near to say those words, somehow you know they're not going to judge you or look down upon you or lecture you. They get it. They don't have to say a word because their simple presence is like a healing ointment to your pain.

So many of my closest friendships today were formed in the midst of a Plan B situation. It's amazing how quickly you can make a deep connection with another person when you share a common struggle.

Me too—it's really a description of one of God's greatest gifts— the gift of community. Dallas Willard describes it this way:

> God's aim in human history is the creation of an all-inclusive commu-
> nity of loving persons with himself included as its primary sustainer
> and most glorious inhabitant. He is even now at work to bring this
> about. You have been invited, at great cost to God himself, to be part
> of this radiant community. You, right there in your life.[2]

But do you *feel* like part of a "radiant community" right there in your life—while you're struggling in a Plan B situation? Are you experiencing the comfort and strength that "me too" can bring?

That's the problem, isn't it? Because when you're in a Plan B, you need community more than ever. And yet, because of the pain that comes along with a Plan B, it's easy to miss the God-given gift of community.

The Gift of Community

I think the book of Ruth is one of the most interesting books of the Bible. It's a book about the subtle ways God can work in the lives of people. It's a book for people who wonder where God is when things are not going as planned, when tragedy after tragedy seems to assault their lives.

In fact, that's exactly where the book of Ruth begins—with the plight of a good woman named Naomi who lives in the land of Judah.

Anyway, Naomi's family is going through a very difficult time.

An economic depression has hit, and her husband loses his liveli-hood. The family ends up losing pretty much everything they have, so out of desperation, they move to a foreign country called Moab.

Now Naomi is not only poor but also living among people who don't speak her language, immersed in a culture that is strange and unfamiliar. The whole situation is a major Plan B for her. But at least she still has all she deeply cares about—her husband and two sons.

That is, until her husband gets sick and dies.

Can you imagine what a blow this is for Naomi? She not only is a stranger in a foreign land but also has lost her partner in life, the love of her life, and her primary means of support. Thank God she has her two sons to walk her through yet another devastating set of circumstances.

Over the next ten years, both her boys marry, and life seems to settle down. Naomi is still a poor widow living in a foreign land, but she finds comfort in her growing family. She gets along well with her new daughters-in-law, Orpah and Ruth, and she's looking forward to being a grandmother some day.

Then, once again, the unthinkable happens. Naomi's two sons, the boys who mean everything to her, also get sick and die.

You can only imagine her screaming and screaming out to God. "Why me? Why me? Why me? How could you let this happen? After all I've been through, God, why me? Why would you take my two boys?"

She has now experienced economic devastation, lost all of her pos-sessions, and been forced to move to a strange land. She's lost her husband and her two sons. She's now a widow living with her two daughters-in-law, who are also widows. She's been stripped of every-thing that could possibly bring her hope. Right?

At the end of her rope, Naomi decides she will now move back to Judah. But she's moving back to nothing. As a widow she has no name, no identity, no rights. She knows she will probably live her life out as a beggar.

Naomi's despair is so deep, in fact, that she changes her name.

In her culture, a name carries a lot of meaning. It symbolizes who a person is. This is why God is always changing people's names in the Bible. A name change signifies that something fundamental has altered in a man or woman's life.

When Naomi gets home, she will tell people, "Don't call me Naomi [which means sweet or pleasant]. Call me Mara [which means bitter], because the Almighty has made my life very sad" (Ruth 1:20).

Who can blame Naomi for having this attitude? She's lost everything that means anything to her. But she hasn't lost her ability to care about others' needs. So before she leaves Moab, she advises her two daughters-in-law, who live with her, to return to their homes and their families and try to rebuild their lives. "You're young. You can find new husbands," she suggests. "Don't tie yourself down to my sad life."

But look at what happens next:

> The women cried together out loud again. Then Orpah kissed her mother-in-law Naomi good-bye, but Ruth held on to her tightly.
>
> Naomi said to Ruth, "Look, your sister-in-law is going back to her own people and her own gods. Go back with her."
>
> But Ruth said, "Don't beg me to leave you or to stop following you. Where you go, I will go. Where you live, I will live. Your people will be my people, and your God will be my God. And where you die, I will die, and there I will be buried . . . Not even death will separate us."
>
> When Naomi saw that Ruth had firmly made up her mind to go with her, she stopped arguing with her. (Ruth 1:11–18)

Here we see the first signs of hope in this story, and it comes through God's gift of community. In Naomi's darkest hour, when all hope has seemingly dissipated, God gives her Ruth. God gives her someone who will say "me too." Someone who knows her pain and loss but can still point her toward the hidden hope in her situation.

Interestingly enough, I don't think Naomi really realizes what a great gift Ruth is. When they return together to Israel, all the women recognize Naomi, and she proceeds to tell them in verse 21, "When I left, I had all I wanted, but now, the LORD has brought me home with nothing." In other words, she's saying, "I have nothing to even live for. Everything I care about is gone." Yet right there with her is Ruth.

At that moment, Naomi is blind to the amazing grace of God in her life. She underestimates just how precious this gift of community is. Why? For the same reason you and I tend to miss God's grace in the midst of our Plan Bs. She had her life scripted, and this is not the way it was supposed to go. So she assumes God has abandoned her and nothing good can happen to her now.

I've watched so many people totally miss God's gift of community in the midst of a Plan B situation because they assumed God wasn't with them. They assumed nothing good could come out of their pain. They failed to appreciate or even recognize the "me too" people who appeared in their lives, offering comfort and strength in the midst of darkness.

And that's a lesson right there for me and for you: don't do it!

Don't allow your pain, as deep as it might be, to keep you from fully embracing the gift of community.

Don't let your disappointment, as devastating as it might be, keep you from hearing (or saying!) "me too."

The Circle Game

I've always said the life of a pastor is an emotional roller coaster. One minute you're on the phone with someone whose father just died; the next minute you are celebrating with a young couple who just got engaged. One hour you're standing in a room surrounded by excited people and leading a prayer for one of your church members who has just opened a new business. The next hour you're standing in a hospital waiting room surrounded by hurting people and leading a prayer for a sixteen-year-old accident victim who is fighting for her life.

And of course, pastors aren't the only ones who experience these roller-coaster dips and climbs. Any of us, at any moment, could be in the winners' circle or the losers' circle. The winners' circle is full of people whose lives in that moment seem to be going just the way they want them. The losers' circle is full of people who are frustrated, hurt, and maybe even angry as they try to figure out why their lives are falling apart in that moment.

This brings up an interesting point. You know, most of my life I've been trying to find my way into winners' circles and stay there as long as I can. I grew up believing that was the goal of life—to make it into the winners' circle where I could celebrate with other winners in life and to avoid the losers' circle if I possibly could.

I think a lot of us grew up with this message, which is powerful in our culture. I also think it's one reason we can miss God's gift of community. It's because we keep looking in all the wrong places for the community we need.

We get this message, I think, not only from the culture we grew up in but also from the church. The cultural idea of the winners' circle tends to involve things such as a nice house, good kids, and a corner office. The church version involves being good, moral, respected, and spiritually successful, implying that only the really committed— the really sold out—ever end up there.

There have been seasons in my life when I've been in winners' circles—both kinds. I can't tell you the deep disappointment I've experienced while there. Winners have the tendency to be shallow, arrogant, and completely dependent on themselves. They are almost always critical and judgmental. There's little giving or sharing. There's little authenticity. And too often you end up feeling as if you just won a bag called success that ended up weighing a ton but was completely empty.

I've also been in enough losers' circles with people who were experiencing pain, hurt, and disappointment to know they tend to be different. While people in the winners' circle are notorious for being judgmental, the broken people in the losers' circle are a little more reluctant to judge. Their Plan Bs have reminded them we all depend upon the mercy of God.

So here's the thing. We're a lot more likely to encounter community in the circle of people who have been broken. But unless we can get the idea out of our heads that winning is the goal of life or the only thing that counts, we're apt to miss the community it offers. Unless we can admit to ourselves that we, too, haven't made it, we're apt to miss the community.

Another way of saying this is that in order to hear a healing "me too," we have to be real about what is going on with us. We have to be *authentic* in order to experience authentic community.

It's authentic community that can usher in healing even in the midst of the most wrenching Plan B circumstances.

False Reality

Why the emphasis on authentic? Because I'm convinced it's largely our inability to be authentic—or real—with each other or ourselves that makes it so difficult for us to recognize the gift of community that God offers us.

The culture we live in today sets up so many expectations for what success looks like. Our Christian communities institute standards that no human being could live up to consistently. So what do we do?

All too often, we hide.

We pretend to be something we're not.

We immerse ourselves in a false reality.

We may "fake it until we make it"—pretending to be a winner even though we suspect we're not. We may cover up our hurt and pain by escaping into addictive behavior. Or we may just get in the habit of not letting anyone—including ourselves—know who we really are or what we're really struggling with.

A couple of years ago, I was at our neighborhood pool with my two oldest boys. It was one of those hot July days when it seemed as if everyone in the subdivision was at the pool. My middle son, Gage, who had a bladder the size of a peanut, came up to me and told me he needed to pee. Again.

Now, please don't judge me for this. But at that moment I was engrossed in a very good book, and in a moment of weakness I told him to just pee in the pool (I know, I know—not my wisest parenting move).

About thirty seconds later, I heard gasps all around the pool. I looked up from my book to see my son Gage standing beside the pool with his trunks around his ankles, urinating into the pool. I threw the book down and yelled, "No, Gage, you can't do that!" By this time everyone around the pool had gotten eerily quiet, so when my son yelled back it echoed: "But Dad, you told me to."

Busted! Boy, was I humiliated. Everyone knew at that moment I didn't belong in the parents' winning circle. And it's a good thing everybody knew who I was that day. Otherwise, I might have just gotten up and walked away, pretending I didn't even know that kid.

"What do you mean I told you to pee in the pool? I've never seen you before in my life."

Well, I'm exaggerating. But I've done just that in an emotional sense, pretending to be something other than what I was. Pretending to be a winner in whatever sense of the word I believed in at the time. Pretending not to care what anyone thinks of me. Pretending I didn't need anybody. Lying to others and to myself about who I am and what is happening to me.

And the more I did this, the further I drifted from living in community with others.

Thomas Merton said, "There is no greater disaster in the spiritual life than to be immersed in unreality, for life is maintained and nourished in us by our vital relation with realities outside and above us."[3] He also said this about our false reality:

> I . . . love . . . to clothe this false self . . . And I wind experiences around myself and cover myself with pleasures and glory like bandages in order to make myself perceptible to myself and to the world, as if I were an invisible body that could only become visible when something visible covered its surface.
>
> But there is no substance under the things with which I am clothed. I am hollow . . . And when they are gone there will be nothing left of me but my own nakedness and emptiness and hollowness.[4]

So many of us fear the nakedness, emptiness, and hollowness of our lives so much we dive headfirst into a pool of unreality. The trouble is, it's only in reality that God meets us, sometimes in very profound ways. And it's only in reality that we can experience true, authentic, healing community with others. So as long as we choose not to live in reality, as long as we insist on covering up our sins and denying them, as long as we keep pretending we have it all together . . . we will probably keep missing the hope that community offers.

We can't benefit from the power of community until we dare to face who we really are.

Someone told me years ago you can only be loved to the extent that you are known. There is so much truth in that. It doesn't matter how many times you tell me you care about me. As long as I have hidden stuff from you, my heart is going to reject your offer of love and friendship. I'll keep thinking, *If you knew the real me, you wouldn't say that.*

It's just a basic fact of life: we can't really experience or appreciate real community until we dare to be authentic. We can't benefit from the power of community until we dare to face who we really are.

The List

Jesus emphasized the importance of authenticity throughout the four gospels. One of my favorite places is found in a parable that tells the story of two men who came to pray:

> Jesus told this story to some people who thought they were very good and looked down on everyone else: "A Pharisee and a tax collector both went to the Temple to pray. The Pharisee stood alone and prayed, 'God, I thank you that I am not like other people who steal, cheat, or take part in adultery, or even like this tax collector. I fast twice a week, and I give one-tenth of everything I get!'" (Luke 18:9–12)

Notice Jesus' comment regarding the posture of the Pharisee. The implication is that the Pharisee wanted to detach himself from the dirty sinners around him. He considers himself superior, and so he wants to separate himself physically from those he considers "unclean."

Then he begins praying, but it's not so much a prayer as a list of all the people who are not in his winners' circle. He gets pretty specific: thieves, cheaters, adulterers, and, of course, tax collectors, who were considered among the lowest of the low in his society.

Now, this list should not be too unfamiliar to you because you have one as well. We all have an unpublished list on our hearts of people we think we're better than.

We don't talk about the list publicly and would be devastated if anyone ever saw it, but the reality is, the list is doing tremendous amounts of damage to our ability to live in the context of community.

For the most part our list of sins generally involves the ones we personally don't struggle with much. You know what sins I think are the most despicable to the heart of God? The ones I don't usually commit. The ones that just don't tempt me—or the ones I fear so much I would never admit. *Those* are the sins on my list, the ones I crusade against.

Seriously. Isn't that what we often do as Christians? We do it in groups too—pointing our collective fingers on one set of "bad" sins and choosing to overlook others.

In other words, it's okay to be prideful as long as you're not gay.

It's okay to be greedy as long as you don't think about having an abortion.

It's okay to be unloving as long as you don't drink.

I'll get off my soapbox here, but let's just be clear. These lists of selective sins and the pride and judgmental attitudes that go with them are ultimately destructive to our spiritual growth. They also obliterate any chances at authentic community. Because it's almost impossible to support and love one another if we can't admit the sins and struggles in our lives. It's almost impossible to receive love and support if we can't even admit that we need it.

You know what sins I think are the most
despicable to the heart of God?
The ones I don't usually commit.
The ones that just don't tempt me—or the ones
I fear so much I would never admit.
Those are the sins on my list,
the ones I crusade against.

You see, it doesn't take long in this story to figure out the Pharisee hasn't really come to the temple to pray. He's actually come to inform God and everyone gathered that particular day of how good he is. He isn't there to seek help and community with other sinners, but to remind them all how self-sufficient he is.

But in that very same place, Jesus tells us, someone else has come to pray. A tax collector—someone on the Pharisee's sin list. And the tax collector's attitude is the complete opposite of the Pharisee's. "The tax collector, standing at a distance, would not even look up to heaven. But he beat on his chest because he was so sad. He said, 'God, have mercy on me, a sinner'" (v. 13).

What a contrast between these two individuals. One is trumpeting his own selected virtues as a way of separating himself from those around him. The other is just being his own broken self, selected sins and all.

And who of the two do you think had a better chance of getting close to God and others?

Authentic Means Surrender

I love being around broken people. Some of the most broken people I've ever spent time with are people battling addictions. I've had a lot of friends find freedom through the famous Twelve Steps of Alcoholics Anonymous. I think there is a lot of biblical truth in those steps.

My friend Jon has been sober for almost ten years now, after decades of addiction to drugs and alcohol. He gives Christ the credit for his freedom. But he also credits the practice of immersing himself in the authentic, broken community that he identifies as his AA group.

One day Jon and I were talking about AA and how it's helped so many people overcome their addictions. "Isn't it ironic," he said, "that one of the most powerful tools against one of the most powerful addictions never asks people to decide to stop doing what it is they have to stop doing?"

I guess I've never really thought about it before, but that really is the way AA works. A Twelve Step program doesn't try to mobilize the addicts' will. It never, ever tells addicts to just suck it up and get over their addictions. The addicts have already tried that—probably hundreds of times—and failed.

Instead, the message of AA is not willpower and self-sufficiency but surrender.

If you're not familiar with the Twelve Step program, the first step states: "We admitted we were powerless over alcohol [or whatever]— that our lives had become unmanageable."[5]

Step three also lends itself toward the practice of surrender. It says, "[We] made a decision to turn our will and our lives over to the care of God *as we understood Him*."[6]

Again, I don't know what your Plan B is. It may or may not have anything to do with an addiction. What I do know is that in the midst of your Plan B, life isn't turning out the way you had hoped. You're being reminded you're not in control, and all of this can lead to some unhealthy extremes.

Here's something else I know. If you try to overcome your Plan B, your problem, your junk, your sin, on your own, it will beat you. Surrender your will, humble yourself, as scary as that is, and then another kind of life becomes possible.

"Have mercy on me, a sinner" are the words that enable you to accept God's forgiveness and comfort. They are also the words that open your ears to hear "me too" from other people around you.

Surrender is essential for you to experience the community you need.

Just read these final words of Jesus in this story. He clearly states the importance of authentic posture before him. He says, "I tell you, when this man went home, he was right with God, but the Pharisee was not. All who make themselves great will be made humble, but all who make themselves humble will be made great" (v. 14).

When we think of surrender, we tend to think of a white flag. We tend to think of loss. However, I believe Scripture teaches that in the end surrender is the only way we can win. It's the only way to be exalted by God himself, and it's the only way we enter into authentic community with each other.

Bring Your Problems

But let's be honest. These moments of authentic surrender like Jesus talks about seem to be rare in the church today. Why is that? Well, this isn't really the purpose of this book, but I think it's a rabbit worth chasing.

I'm afraid there is a pervasive assumption in some Christian circles that once you give your life to Christ, once you've become a Christian, you need to at least act like you've got it together. I remember once hearing pastor Matt Chandler describe it like this: "We want you to bring your Bible, but not your problems."

Isn't that an unfortunate word picture to describe so many of our churches? Bring your Bible, bring your religion, bring your mask, look pretty. But whatever you do, don't be a whiner. Don't ask questions, don't be a pain, don't be a burden. This attitude is a community killer, and it's doing immense damage to the body of Christ.

I'm not sure exactly where this attitude comes from, but I think it originates with fear. We don't want people to share their broken dreams, hurts, and their pain because we're afraid we won't have the answers. Even worse, we might have to face our own brokenness instead of pretending we're headed for the winners' circle.

Regardless of its origins, the result is clear. People in churches often fail to bring their real problems to church. So often in our churches we don't hear about stuff until it's too late. It's as though nobody has small problems.

As someone once described it to me, we only hear about the house burning down; we don't hear about the electrical problem.

We hear about the divorce . . . but what if they could have shared about the pornography issue?

We hear that they're going to prison for embezzlement . . . but what if they could have shared about the overwhelming financial problems?

We hear about the suicides . . . but what if they could have shared the overwhelming darkness that was closing in around them?

We hear that their son ran away from home . . . but what if they would have shared all the conflict they were having up to that point?

We'll never know what might have happened if people had been able to open their lives up enough to hear—and to say—"me too."

There is no doubt that sometimes Christian community can be a dangerous place when your dreams shatter. Christians (like other sinners) can be guilty of clichéd answers, untruthful promises, and false expectations. Christians (like other sinners) have been known to be judgmental or simply oblivious. Christians (like other sinners) often neglect to say "me too" or even to acknowledge that it's possible.

So if you're tempted to run away from church or just cover up your hurt while you're with other people, I can understand. But I hope you won't do that. I'd like to encourage you to fight the temptation to hide. Take the risk of sharing your authentic self whenever you can possibly manage it. Trust that God will eventually provide you with a community that will circle around you even if this comes from the most unlikely of places. (In the process, you may be a true godsend for someone else who is hurting and in need of hearing "me too.")

Together

The apostle Paul gives us a moving picture of what Christian community *should* look like when he writes, "By helping each other with your troubles, you truly obey the law of Christ" (Gal. 6:2). But we can't help each other with troubles until we make those troubles known to the community. We must get to a place where we get past our pride and freely present our needs to the community around us. In essence, we need to confess like the psalmist did in Psalm 142:6:

> *Listen to my cry,*
> *because I am helpless.*

Crack Granny

I met Sheila for the first time when I was leaving work late one evening. It was dark, and she scared me as she came around the corner on her bike.

"Hey, I need some money," she said. "Would you give me some money?"

I asked her, "What do you need some money for?"

She said, "I'm homeless, and I need some food."

Well, Sheila wasn't lying about being homeless, but she was lying about the food. She was begging for money so she could feed her addictions—addictions that had raged in her life for decades. On any given day, she could be riding her bike up and down the street, begging for money and offering her body for sex—often for as little as ten dollars. She was a somewhat infamous character in the neighborhood where our Cross Point campus sits. She even had a nickname: Crack Granny.

Almost every day, someone from our staff would have a conversation with Sheila. Usually it consisted of her following us to one of our cars, telling lies and trying to con one of us for money. Eventually though, Ryan Bult, our pastor of missions, broke through her rough, manipulative exterior and started to build a relationship with her. Over time, she started to be open and real with several of us about her issues, and we started to put the pieces of her story together—a story of one Plan B crisis after another.

Sheila had grown up in an abusive home. Both of her parents, who were also alcoholics, had died before she was even a teenager. At age thirteen she had started experimenting with alcohol and drugs. For the next thirty-seven years, she abused any substance she could get her hands on—booze, pot, pills, and eventually crack.

She told me once, "Pete, I had a gnawing on the inside of me. There was never one second of one day that I can remember not being consumed with getting my next hit. I put myself in a lot of dangerous situations, especially with men. I didn't care how much money they gave me or how they treated me. I just wanted my next hit."

One day I asked Sheila why she finally started opening up to Ryan. She said, "Well, I just couldn't believe someone wanted to listen to me. He wouldn't preach at me or put me down. He just talked to me like a regular person, and it made me feel good."

Clearly, having a friend she could talk to was a big deal for Sheila. Years of abuse from those she loved and from many she didn't even know had made it very difficult for her to imagine she could ever live in open, authentic community with others. It was difficult for her to imagine that anyone could really love the real Sheila.

Though it was wonderful for all of us to see Sheila beginning to open up to us, for a very long time we saw very little change in her patterns of behavior. To be honest, we found this a little frustrating. But we were committed to providing a place where she could belong before she believed, so we kept on reaching out to her.

Then came a defining moment. In the winter of 2008, Sheila had a massive heart attack and died. Miraculously, some five minutes later, doctors were able to revive her lifeless body.

Sheila would later say that she believed God was giving her not just a second chance but a last chance—a chance to finally stop running from her painful past and surrender her life to Christ. And that is exactly what she did. With the help of Ryan and others from our Cross Point community, she began to understand what it meant to receive grace and forgiveness at the foot of the cross—and to open her life to community.

From that point on, Sheila's life really began to turn around. Ryan and others from Cross Point got her into treatment programs for her addictions. They also helped her get off the streets by finding an apartment for her and then furnishing it.

It's been amazing to have a front-row seat to the transformation that has begun to take place in Sheila's life. As she has learned to walk with God and the people he has placed in her life, I've seen a sparkle in her eyes I didn't see before. For the first time in thirty-seven years, she is free from the demons that held her mind and body hostage.

Just last week I walked out into our church lobby to find Sheila sitting at a table with the wife of a successful builder, a man who is paralyzed from the waist down as a result of a stroke, a homeless man, a woman addicted to crystal meth, and a local businessman. This group gathers every Thursday to fold programs for our Cross Point church services. As they fold, they share struggles, highlights, and what's going on in their lives in general. Every time I walk by this group, I'm reminded of the incredible power of the gospel—and the power of community.

Sheila used to show up at our door to see what she could get. Now she shows up to see how she can give. And she is no longer Crack Granny. She is now Sheila, a child of God, forgiven, set free, and part of a loving, embracing community. But this healing in her life has only been possible because she took a risk. She stepped out of her comfort zone and stopped running long enough to recognize that God was sending a group of people into her life to help her with her troubles.

Two Are Better Than One

The writer of Ecclesiastes wisely observes:

> *Two people are better than one,*
> *because they get more done by working together.*
> *If one falls down,*
> *the other can help him up.*
> *But it is bad for the person who is alone and falls,*
> *because no one is there to help.*
> *If two lie down together, they will be warm,*
> *but a person alone will not be warm.*
> *An enemy might defeat one person,*
> *but two people together can defend themselves;*
> *a rope that is woven of three strings is hard to break. (Eccles. 4:9–12)*

In the midst of our Plan B we desperately need a community pledged to build each other up and to watch out for each other's good. Paul urges, "We who are strong in faith should help the weak with their weaknesses, and not please only ourselves " (Rom. 15:1).

This kind of community is indispensable when it feels as if your life is falling apart.

Having personally watched hundreds of people go through Plan Bs, I would say one of the single most important factors in whether we lean on God or not is the group of people we have around us. Separated from community, we tend to think the worst. Separated from community, we tend to tilt toward hopelessness. And while authentic community doesn't take away the pain in the midst of a Plan B, it certainly helps reframe the pain.

The only thing worse than disappointment is disappointment without a community. It's disappointment with a community that can help guide you toward a hope anchored in our God.

Philip Yancey says that "God's presence often comes as a by-product of other people's presence."[7] I've personally experienced many moments in the midst of Plan Bs where God's presence was most evident by the community he had placed around me. However, the benefits of this community always came *after* I took the risk of opening up my life to others.

Separated from community, we tend to think the worst. Separated from community, we tend to tilt toward hopelessness. And while authentic community doesn't take away the pain in the midst of a Plan B, it certainly helps reframe the pain.

It's really your choice. You can continue to try to mask the pain. You can grow bitter and lonely, feeling as if you're all alone in the midst of your Plan B. Or you can open your eyes as Naomi eventually did. (Read the book of Ruth to find out how!) You can take a risk as Sheila did. Begin to trust and believe that maybe, just maybe, there is someone in your life who can and will speak those healing words, "me too."

TEN THE ANCHOR

Here's where I think we start to turn a corner in this book—a corner that may be difficult for you to turn. This chapter may be tough to read. But if I just tell you what you want to hear, I just wrote this book about me, and not about God and what he wants to do in our lives.

It's about the reality of what God has done for us and what we have done to him.

It's about the cross.

Not the cross we often have hanging in our churches but that rough instrument of torture that Jesus died on. Not the cross we hang around our necks (in gold or silver or pewter) but that agonizing event that shook the world.

Look at the darkness of the cross.

Look at the confusion of the cross.

Look at the tragedy of the cross.

Jurgen Moltmann writes:

The cross is the utterly incommensurable factor in the revelation of God. We have become far too used to it. We have surrounded the scandal of the cross with roses. Here the faith in creation, the source of all paganism, breaks down. Here this whole philosophy and wisdom is abandoned to folly. Here God is non-God. Here is the triumph of death, the enemy, the non-church, the lawless state, the blasphemer, the soldiers. Here Satan triumphs over God. Our faith begins at the point where atheists suppose that it must be at the end. Our faith begins with the bleakness and power which is the night of the cross, abandonment, temptation, and doubt about everything that exists![1]

Do you see what this means? Our very faith is born out of uncertainty, darkness, and despair. It's out of this seeming tragedy, this ultimate Plan B, that something amazing and transformational is born.

That's what the cross tells us.

And it tells us something more. It tells us some important things about ourselves and our Plan B situations.

Fruit Snacks

The other day my wife got a rare opportunity to go out with some friends, and I got the opportunity to hang out with our three boys for the day. While I think I'm a pretty good dad and can do an adequate job of herding our guys, Brandi usually leaves me a cheat sheet when she's going to be gone for a while. The cheat sheet reminds me of naptimes, suggests food options, and even gives medical instructions. I don't know that it's needed, but I have to admit it gives me a sense of comfort.

Brewer, our two-year-old, loves to snack. He can eat his weight in those synthetic fruit snacks that are actually just gummy worms shaped like fruit. Somehow the fruit shapes make you feel better as a parent and you actually start to think you're giving your children a healthy snack, even though that particular snack contains zero healthy ingredients.

We were having a great day together until I decided it was time to cut Brewer off from the fruit snacks. I was convinced that if he ate one more pack he could possibly explode internally.

When I denied him that next pack, all hell broke loose. He went nuts on me, running through the house and screaming, "I want Mommy! I want Mommy! I want Mommy!"

I remember thinking, *Oh, and I want your mommy too. I would love nothing more than for your mommy to walk through this door right now.*

Over and over again he screamed, "I want Mommy! I want Mommy!"

You know what? He didn't really want Mommy. He wanted what he thought Mommy could give him.

Now, let's hit the pause button for just a second. Can we be real with each other? At the risk of you closing the book right here, I think you might need to hear something. You may be at odds with God right now. You're not happy with the way your life is turning out. You may be praying and pleading with God.

But is it possible you don't really want God?

Is it possible you just want what you think God can give you?

One of the things I believe God is teaching me in my life these days is that at times we want our dreams more than we want God. We want what God does for us instead of just God.

Is it possible you don't really want God?
Is it possible you just want what you think
God can give you?

Maybe that's why this passage from Exodus 33 resonates with me so much:

Then the LORD said to Moses, "You and the people you brought out of Egypt must leave this place. Go to the land that I promised with an oath to give to Abraham, Isaac, and Jacob when I said, 'I will give that land to your descendants.' I will send an angel to lead you, and I will force these people out of the land: the Canaanites, Amorites, Hittites, Perizzites, Hivites, and Jebusites." (vv. 1–2)

Did you get that? God promises Moses success in battle, success in claiming the promised land for his people. This is what Moses has wanted all along, right? This is the dream he's been pursuing ever since he left Egypt.

However, Moses responds to God's promise in a surprising way:

Moses said to the LORD, "You have told me to lead these people, but you did not say whom you would send with me. You have said to me, 'I know you very well, and I am pleased with you.' If I have truly pleased you, show me your plans so that I may know you and continue to please you. Remember that this nation is your people."

The LORD answered, "I myself will go with you, and I will give you victory."

Then Moses said to him, "If you yourself don't go with us, then don't send us away from this place. If you don't go with us, no one will know that you are pleased with me and with your people. These people and I will be no different from any other people on earth."

Then the LORD said to Moses, "I will do what you ask, because I know you very well, and I am pleased with you." (Exod. 33:12–17)

I love this. Moses is saying, "God, success is not enough for me. I want you. I want your presence. I don't just want what you can give me. I want you."

I'm desperately trying to get to a place where I believe this truth to my core. I want to reach the point that I can honestly say, "If God doesn't give me one more thing in this life, I still owe him everything."

Difficult Questions

We have been asking some difficult questions in this book, questions such as "What do you do with a shattered dream?", "What do you do with an unmet expectation?", and "What do you do when God doesn't show up for you the way you thought God was going to show up?"

More specifically, what do you do when your marriage falls apart, when you find out you have Alzheimer's, when you lose a loved one, or when a close friend betrays you?

I don't know if I can give you a specific answer in any of those circumstances, but here is what I do know. I've said it throughout this book, and I'll say it again. We all are going to get to that place where life hurts and our hearts are broken. We all are going to find ourselves in the middle of a Plan B. And here's the addition that may shock you: being a Christian doesn't change this reality at all.

Please hear me. I'm not saying that being a Christian doesn't make a difference in our lives. I'm just saying that Christianity cannot always be reduced to simple answers.

Perhaps you thought that when you became a Christian you would have all the answers to life's difficulties. But here is a reality check and, hopefully, a pressure release for you. Being a Christian doesn't mean you know how to respond to everything that comes your way. Being a Christian doesn't mean you have all the answers!

I'm so frustrated with the version of Christianity where we actually think our theology can fit onto a bumper sticker, a T-shirt, or a bracelet. Reality just isn't that simple. The reality is:

- Christians often have more questions than answers.
- Sometimes we lack the faith that gives us sustained hope.
- Even though we know God is with us, sometimes we feel utterly and completely alone.

- Even though we believe, we doubt.
- And even when we suspect God knows what he is doing, we really don't want to do things his way.

I'm so frustrated with the version of Christianity
where we actually think our theology can fit onto
a bumper sticker, a T-shirt, or a bracelet.
Reality just isn't that simple.

In Him

I think Jesus understood better than any of us just how complex and confusing all of this would be. In John 16 he speaks about two realities you and I need to come to grips with if we are ever going to make sense of our Plan B seasons in life.

Quick background: Jesus is about to be crucified. He's headed for the cross. He is carrying the sins of the world, and he is going to the cross so we can experience forgiveness and redemption through his substitutionary death. In other words, he's getting ready to pay a penalty that was ours to pay. And this is what he tells his followers: "I told you these things so that you can have peace in me. In this world you will have trouble, but be brave! I have defeated the world" (John 16:33).

Anyone interested in this peace he offers? Notice he says, "you can have peace in me." I think those words "in me" are really important. Jesus doesn't say we'll have peace in church . . . or in a small group . . . or in this book.

He clearly says, "in me." When you immerse your current reality into his reality, that is where peace is found.

The very next words out of Jesus' mouth remind us just why this peace is so important. He says, "In this world you will have trouble."

That is Jesus' way of saying, "You're really going to need peace because trouble is coming." (You might say, "Well, duh.")

And we are not talking about my-dog-pooped-on-the-floor trouble or I-locked-myself-out-of-my-house trouble or I'm-stuck-in-a-traffic-jam kind of trouble. We're talking about the kind of trouble that makes you think, *I don't know if there is a God. I don't know if I believe anymore.* This is the kind of trouble, pain, or crisis that can rock you to your very core.

You can almost picture Jesus in this verse as a weather forecaster who is giving us the seven-day outlook. It's trouble, trouble, trouble, trouble, trouble, trouble, and trouble. In a word, the forecast for your life here on this earth is *trouble*.

This is true because we are living in two overlapping realities:

- There is a God who is big and powerful and loves us . . .
- . . . but we live in a world that seems to be falling apart.

And then Jesus ends this verse by saying, "But be brave! I have defeated the world." In other words, "Don't lose sight of the big picture. Don't give in to despair. Because I've already done what is necessary to eventually take care of all the trouble you will have. No matter what comes, I have defeated the world."

Bad Theology

It's interesting, but this one verse can spawn some really jacked-up theologies. I heard pastor Louie Giglio talk about this verse. He helped it come alive for me in a time in my life when I desperately needed it.[2] It was right after Brandi and I had experienced our first miscarriage, and I was struggling with how this could have happened to our family.

Giglio pointed out that there are really two parts to John 16:33.

First, Jesus clearly says that we're going to have trouble in this world. Then he tells us to be brave because he has defeated the world. Two statements—and if you separate them, you have two bad theologies.

For instance, if you just focus on Jesus' first statement, "in this world you will have trouble" (NIV), you could develop a mental framework of "this world stinks." Stuff happens, and you can't do a thing about it. You live, and then you die.

I'm sure you've met people who have chosen this framework for their thinking. They always feel like someone or something is out to destroy them. They feel life is pointless. It's a pretty miserable way to live.

But what if you focus only on the second half of this verse, where Jesus says, "I have overcome the world" (NIV)? If you take just this statement as a mental framework, you start to think there will never be any trouble—or at least no serious trouble. "Nothing bad is going to happen to me as long as I'm following Jesus." If you cling only to this statement, you force yourself to live in a false reality. Despite all evidence to the contrary, you just pretend everything is great and all the charts of your life are going to keep moving up and to the right. In the process, you're probably setting yourself up for a fall because your false reality will eventually be shattered.

But if you take the two statements in this verse and put them together, then you have what Jesus was talking about. You have a more complete theology.

You are not exempt from trouble, even serious trouble. You are not exempt from Plan Bs. But at the same time, you can have confidence that Jesus will win out over trouble. In that there is hope.

But you might be saying, "Well, Pete, how do you know that?"

I know this because of the cross and what it communicates to all of humankind.

The Cross

Now, you may say, "No, you don't understand. I'm already a Christian. I've already done my business at the cross. I have already been forgiven. I don't need the cross. What I need is for you to talk about solutions. I need you to talk about steps. I need you to talk about the future. How do I move on from here?"

I think this is a common mistake we make in Christianity today. We view the cross as the starting line. Once we've accepted Christ's forgiveness, provided through the cross, we want to move on.

But it doesn't work that way. You need to know the cross is not just the starting line. It's the very centerpiece of your story with God.

It's the place where the pain of "you will have trouble" meets the triumph of "I have defeated the world."

And it's the reason we can have hope even in the midst of our Plan B situations.

The author of Hebrews says this about God's promises: "We have this hope as an anchor for the soul, sure and strong. It enters behind the curtain in the Most Holy Place in heaven" (Heb. 6:19).

> You need to know the cross is not just the starting line. It's the very centerpiece of your story with God. It's the place where the pain of "you will have trouble" meets the triumph of "I have defeated the world."

I'm not sure there is anything you need more in this unpredictable world than an anchor. Do you feel as if you're being banged around by the sea of life? Do you feel as if you're just aimlessly drifting? What you need is an anchor—an anchor of hope.

I believe the cross can be and should be that anchor. You see, the cross is not something that just gets you into heaven. Its also the stabilizing force you need when your world is turbulent from a Plan B or a series of Plan Bs.

God's Love

Over the next couple of chapters, I want to talk about what the cross means to us, and I want to start by talking about the love it communicates.

Understanding and grasping God's unending love is essential in the midst of any Plan B. It's essential because it's so easy to assume, *God must not love me if he is letting me go through this. God must have abandoned me, or I wouldn't be feeling this way.*

If we simply focus on circumstances and if we define God through those circumstances, that conclusion seems to make sense. But when we get our eyes on the cross, we are reminded that there are no limits to what God will do to draw us to him. We are reminded that God does love us more than we could ever imagine.

The knowledge of God's love is not going to make the pain of Plan B go away. But we can allow his love to become the fuel that sustains us through the long, difficult days ahead.

When our lives are being rocked by this broken world, we need to look to the cross as a reminder that God can and will redeem our circumstances. God does love us, and that supersedes whatever Plan B situation we might be going through.

What Is Your Idol?

The trouble is, we don't always manage to do that.

The trouble is, we're often tempted to take our eyes from the loving reality of the cross and look for other ways of coping with the pain of our Plan B situations. One of the most common forms of temptations is the practice of idolatry.

And no, I don't mean we pull out the old woodcarving tools and put together something we can literally bow down to.

My favorite definition of idolatry is simply to take something other than God and make it our ultimate focus. We make it the most important thing in our lives and pursue it at all costs. We depend on it to give us good things and help us out of bad situations. Do you see what I mean? When you look at it this way . . .

- Money can be an idol. (It's a popular one.)
- Technology can be an idol. (It's getting bigger by the day.)
- Acceptance can be an idol. (This one is big in high schools and corporations.)
- Family can even be an idol. (Ouch!)

Idolatry was exactly what Satan was trying to tempt Jesus with in Matthew 4. Do you remember that story? Because Jesus was hungry and thirsty, Satan tempted him with offers of food and drink . . . and the possibility of calling angels and taking the easy way out of what he was on earth for. But then Satan pulled out the big guns of idolatry. He tried to allure Jesus by saying, in effect, "Look at all the kingdoms in the world. I can give them to you. Look at what you could have if you would just worship me. You could have 'all of this' if you would only worship me and adore me. Let me drive your life."

Jesus, of course, said no.

We don't always manage to do that.

Now, you may be wondering what idolatry has to do with your Plan B, but just hang with me for a minute here. I want to take you to a somewhat obscure text to show you what I'm talking about. It's from the book of Ezekiel, and it uses a completely different word picture to talk about the ways we tend to act toward God and the way God looks at us. In this passage, God is talking to Jerusalem—who represents us:

> "Later when I passed by you and looked at you, I saw that you were old enough for love. So I spread my robe over you and covered your nakedness. I also made a promise to you and entered into an agreement with you so that you became mine, says the Lord GOD" (Ezek. 16:8)

Kind of racy, isn't it? It's intended to be. You have to understand this is a poetic foreshadowing of God's relationship with us. The idea is that God loves us so much that he actually enters into a covenant of marriage with us. "I spread the corner of my garment over you and covered your nakedness." The symbolic act of spreading the lower part of one's garment over another signifies protection and betrothal or commitment.

In this passage, God tells how he pledged his fidelity to Jerusalem (us again) and took her as his own. He continues:

> "Then I bathed you with water, washed all the blood off of you, and put oil on you. I put beautiful clothes made with needlework on you and put sandals of fine leather on your feet. I wrapped you in fine linen and covered you with silk. I put jewelry on you: bracelets on your arms, a necklace around your neck, a ring in your nose, earrings in your ears, and a beautiful crown on your head. So you wore gold and silver. Your clothes were made of fine linen, silk, and beautiful needlework. You ate fine flour, honey, and olive oil. You were very beautiful and became a queen. Then you became famous among the nations, because you were so beautiful. Your beauty was perfect, because of the glory I gave you, says the Lord GOD." (vv. 9–14)

In other words, when we entered into a relationship with God, he covered our sin and made us beautiful and presentable. He adorned us with his grace and filled us with his beauty—all because he loves us. But then this happened:

> "But you trusted in your beauty. You became a prostitute, because you were so famous. You had sexual relations with anyone who passed by. You took some of your clothes and made your places of worship colorful. There you carried on your prostitution. These things should not happen; they should never occur. You also took your beautiful jewelry, made from my gold and silver I had given you, and you made for yourselves male idols so you could be a prostitute with them. Then you took your clothes with beautiful needlework and covered the idols. You gave my oil and incense as an offering to them. Also, you took the bread I gave you, the fine flour, oil, and honey I gave you to eat, and you offered them before the gods as a pleasing smell. This is what happened, says the Lord GOD." (Ezek. 16:15–19)

Can you believe what this passage is saying? It's basically calling me and you—as part of Christ's body, as part of the church—a prostitute, a whore. Then it goes on to say that not only am I a whore, but I'm a spiritual nymphomaniac, who actually pays men to sleep with me as opposed to just taking their money. That is the language that Scripture uses to talk about the hearts of God's people—how adulterous we are and how idolatrous and spiritually wrecked we are.

Not Me

"Well, that's not me," you may say. "I'm not a whore. I haven't cheated on God."

But let's think about this for a moment. I think all of us have at least one area of our lives where we're tempted to pursue something other than God.

Maybe for you it's something traditionally considered "bad"—like alcohol or drugs or pornography. More likely, it's not something so glaringly destructive. It may even be something that can be somewhat morally neutral or permissible—until it becomes an idol.

So how do you know where and what you worship? Louie Giglio suggests you have to follow the trails in your life.[3] Follow the trail of your . . .

- Time—how you spend most of the hours of your day (working, watching TV, gardening, goofing off on the Internet)
- Affections—what you care most about, what relationships you nurture (your spouse, your children, your pets, your church friends)
- Energy—what you work and play hardest at (the gym, your job, hobbies, avocations, helping people)
- Money—what your bank statement indicates about where your money goes (saving for the future, eating out, toys and entertainment, helping your children, tithing)
- Allegiance—what you're most loyal to (your church, your job, your family, yourself)

Follow the trail of all these things. At the end of that trail you'll find a throne; and whatever—or whomever—is on that throne is what's of highest value to you. It's your ultimate . . . your idol . . . your adulterous lover.

Not many of us walk around saying, "I worship my stuff. I worship my job. I worship this pleasure. I worship her. I worship my body. I worship my dream." But the trail never lies. In the end our worship, our idolatry, is more about what we do than what we say.

And I think for those of us in the midst of a Plan B we'll discover that one of our idols all along has been a picture of the way life should be. Our idol was an expectation or a dream.

Worthless Gods

And here's what God, who loves us, has to say about the ways we chase after idols:

> "I will also hand you over to your lovers. They will tear down your places of worship and destroy other places where you worship gods. They will tear off your clothes and take away your jewelry, leaving you naked and bare. They will bring a crowd against you to throw stones at you and to cut you into pieces with their swords. They will burn down your houses and will punish you in front of many women. I will put an end to your sexual sins, and you will no longer pay your lovers. Then I will rest from my anger against you, and I will stop being jealous. I will be quiet and not angry anymore." (Ezek. 16:39–42)

In other words God is saying, "If it's these other lovers you really want, then I'll allow you to chase after them. I'll hand you over to them, but you need to know they will hurt and damage you."

You can give your love and devotion to climbing the ladder, but eventually that lover will crush you.

You can give your love and devotion to amassing wealth, but eventually that lover will betray you.

You can give your love and devotion to gaining acceptance, but eventually that lover will shatter you.

You can give your love and devotion to a particular dream, but eventually that lover will disappoint you.

It's possible, in other words, that part of the reason you feel so shattered and so broken in the midst of your Plan B situations is that you gave your love and devotion to your plans and dreams instead of God.

It's something to keep in mind. Because no matter how worthy, no matter how compelling, no matter how *good*—a dream makes a worthless god.

Not My Dream

Jesus himself modeled for us this very principle of not worshiping your dreams and plans over God. It happens on the night before his death, when he goes to a garden with his followers to pray:

> He said to them, "Sit here while I go over there and pray." He took Peter and the two sons of Zebedee with him, and he began to be very sad and troubled. He said to them, "My heart is full of sorrow, to the point of death. Stay here and watch with me."
>
> After walking a little farther away from them, Jesus fell to the ground and prayed, "My Father, if it is possible, do not give me this cup of suffering. But do what you want, not what I want." (Matt. 26:36–39)

I think some of us are so familiar with this text we actually miss the emotion being conveyed here. Read it again. Jesus is so "full of sorrow" that he falls to the ground. He's facing the ultimate Plan B, and he's in so much emotional pain about it that he literally cannot walk.

Am I suggesting that Jesus doesn't know he is going to the cross? No, I think he clearly knows what's about to happen. He knows exactly what's going to happen, in fact—the pain, the humiliation, the death. And as he faces that prospect, he pleads and begs for another way. *God, please, I don't know if I can do this. I'm overwhelmed just thinking about it.*

Then Jesus went back to his followers and found them asleep. He said to Peter, "You men could not stay awake with me for one hour? Stay awake and pray for strength against temptation. The spirit wants to do what is right, but the body is weak." Then Jesus went away a second time and prayed, "My Father, if it is not possible for this painful thing to be taken from me, and if I must do it, I pray that what you want will be done." (vv. 40–42)

Those final words of Jesus are the most important words for us to learn to say and believe to our core. Jesus said, "I pray that what you want will be done." In other words, he's saying, "I don't like this, I wish there was another way, and I'm not even sure I can handle this. But it's not about my dreams, my desires, my plans. It's not about my will but your will, so let it be so in my life." Jesus refused to allow his dreams, his expectations, or his will to become his idols.

That's what we're called to do, too, especially in those times when our Plan B situations expose the idols we are chasing.

We must be willing, if necessary, to abandon the life we've planned and dreamed of in order to receive the life that our God has authored for us.

And we must keep our eyes on the cross, remembering that our faith is born out of darkness and confusion. Remembering that trouble is a given in this world, but that Jesus has defeated the world. Remembering that God has been faithful to us and demands our allegiance in return, that he wants us to pursue him even over our dreams and desires (which we've seen make lousy gods).

But remembering most of all—in the midst of the darkness and confusion of Plan B—that God is our passionate Lover, willing to go to extreme limits and pay a huge cost so that we can enter into relationship with him.

God loves us—that's our anchor of hope in the turbulence of Plan B.

God loves us—that's the message of the cross that changes everything.

Absolutely everything.

ELEVEN POWER AND HOPE

I'd like you to take just a moment to imagine yourself on the scene where Jesus was crucified. Just think for a second what it must have been like at the cross.

People are screaming and crying. People are cheering and chanting and jeering. Certain leaders are manipulating the crowd. Soldiers are abusing the Son of God. Soldiers are gambling over his clothes. A thief hanging next to Jesus is making fun of him. Then things get really crazy:

> It was about noon, and the whole land became dark until three o'clock in the afternoon, because the sun did not shine. The curtain in the Temple was torn in two. Jesus cried out in a loud voice, "Father, I give you my life." After Jesus said this, he died. When the army officer there saw what happened, he praised God, saying, "Surely this was a good man!" (Luke 23:44–47)

If you just happened to be there on that day, you would have to say, "This is horrible. Where is God in the midst of all of this? This is out of control!"

And yet it was not. God was not absent even in the midst of that chaotic scene. God was not out of control—which can be helpful to remember in the midst of your own Plan B chaos.

Because your situation does feel out of control, doesn't it? You can't believe what happened—can't believe . . .

- he walked out on you.
- the treatment isn't working.
- your savings really are gone.
- your child is in jail.

And if you're honest, you don't have a clue what to do about the situation. You don't know . . .

- how to get out of trouble.
- how to feel better.
- how to talk about it.
- how to get well.
- how to make amends.

Whatever your particular problems, you're not sure if there's a way past them. You're convinced life will never be the same, and you're pretty sure it will never be good again.

But can you believe God is in control now, even when your life isn't?

If you can hold on to that, you'll have absorbed another important gift of the cross. Something that has to do with power and control . . . but has even more to do with hope.

Can you believe God is in control now,
even when your life isn't?

Superheroes

Growing up, like most average kids, I used to fantasize about being a superhero. Did you have a superhero you admired? I always thought I wanted to be Superman. I wanted to be able to run like he could run. I wanted to be able to fly like he could fly. I wanted his power, his courage, and his desire to make a difference. Okay, and I wanted the really cool outfit too.

I was talking with my oldest son, Jett, one day and asked him, "Son, if you could have any superpower, what power would you want?" He sat there for a moment, contemplating his answer, and then said, "I want the power to not ever have to go pee."

What? Of all the superpowers available, he wanted the power to be able to hold his bladder?

He said, "Yeah, Dad. Think of all the time I could save. I'd never have to stop playing to go inside and pee."

Trying to think of something to say, I just muttered, "Son, I think that is the lamest superpower I've ever heard of. What is your name going to be? No-Pee Man? Super Bladder Dude? You've got to come up with something better than that, Son. What are you going to do with that kind of power, buddy? Bust in to save the girl and say, 'Everyone step back. I don't have to pee.'"?

Okay, I'll let it go.

But I think there is a reason we're so fascinated with superheroes. On the surface it has to do with power. I don't care who you talk to these days, we all feel a little powerless, a little out of control. We could all use a power beyond ourselves.

But I think there's a little more to our yearning than a need for power.

I suspect what we really need is hope.

Power just happens to be the tool we think we need to defeat the things in this world that are standing in the way of our hope.

That's why people who have lost hope will often say, "I just feel so powerless."

We could all use a power beyond ourselves.
But I think there's a little more to our yearning than a
need for power. I suspect what we really need is hope.

Hope is what we desire. It's what we all desperately need. And when we're going through a Plan B circumstance, whatever the specific Plan B might be, hope often feels scarce.

State of Shock

It obviously felt that way to the disciples who stood in that chaotic scene beside the cross. Because look how they responded:

> When all the people who had gathered there to watch saw what happened, they returned home, beating their chests because they were so sad. But those who were close friends of Jesus, including the women who had followed him from Galilee, stood at a distance and watched. (Luke 23:48–49)

Those who bought into the mission of Jesus, who believed he was the Son of God, can't believe what they were seeing. They've hung all their hope on this man named Jesus. And at this one moment their entire hope is dying on a cross.

Again, the whole scene must feel totally out of control. People are upset, angry, and confused.

But notice how Jesus' closest followers react. The gospel account says they "stood at a distance and watched."

Think about that. Other people are walking away, beating their chests. But Jesus' closest friends aren't doing anything. They're just . . . standing . . . there.

Have you ever been so hopeless you can't do a thing? You can't get mad or fight or even cry? You feel so hopeless you don't have the energy or passion to even get ticked off.

When I was pastoring in Kentucky, I would often ride with law-enforcement officials after someone had been murdered or killed in a car accident. The officers liked having me along when they went to inform the next of kin. I still remember the sick feeling I would get when we pulled into a driveway to do that sad job. I would think, *Inside that house is a family just living their life, going through their normal routine. They have no idea how my next few words are going to turn their very life upside down forever.*

I always found it interesting how people responded when we informed them of their loved one's death. I always expected a lot of emotion—screaming and crying and such. But often they reacted in the same way the Bible says Jesus' close followers responded. They were so overwhelmed they just stood there. Sometimes they would fall to the ground unable to speak, unable to cry, unable to really respond at all.

That's exactly how Jesus' group of close followers responded to his death. These were people who loved him and shared life with him. They bought into his vision. They had dreams—some realistic, some not so much—that were tied up with Jesus' ministry. I can assure you watching the crucifixion of Jesus felt like a major dream killer for them, the ultimate Plan B. They felt all they had worked for, all they had trusted, was slipping away. This out-of-control, helpless feeling put them in a state of shock.

Helpless and Hopeless

Let's be honest. We all have these dreams, we have these thoughts, we have these plans, but we lack the power to be who we want to be and do what we want to do. Lacking the power to execute our dreams seems to be the human condition.

You may be in that hopeless state. Your dreams have come crashing down around you, but you're no longer complaining.

You're not crying.

You're not fighting.

You've kind of accepted defeat. You're overcome with hopelessness.

Maybe you had a vocational dream you thought for sure was going to happen—but for one reason or another, it didn't. So you've given up and settled for less than you desire.

Maybe you had dreams for your marriage, but it's so overwhelmed with mediocrity you've given up. You used to fight for a good marriage, but now you feel like there's no point. Nothing's going to change.

Maybe you just had the dream of being married. You were sure you'd be living that dream by now, but you feel all alone. You've given up on finding that guy or that girl.

Maybe you had dreams for your kids. You were positive they would turn out this way or that way, but they've taken a different path from what you expected. Maybe your kids are so out of control you're not even trying anymore. You've lost hope in what they can be.

Whatever your particular Plan B, you've run out of faith in possibilities. You've run out of energy for trying something new. You know you're not in control, and deep in your heart, you're not sure that God is, either.

If that's where you are, I'd like to offer a word of hope.

I'd like to suggest that things may not be as bad as they feel.

When Hope Is Dead

Here's what happens after the unthinkable happened, after Jesus' disciples watched him die in agony and watched their dreams die (they assume) with him:

Joseph went to Pilate to ask for the body of Jesus. He took the body down from the cross, wrapped it in cloth, and put it in a tomb that was cut out of a wall of rock. This tomb had never been used before. This was late [in the day], and when the sun went down, the Sabbath day would begin. (Luke 23:52–54)

And that's that.

For more than a day, from sundown on Friday (when the Sabbath began) to until early Sunday morning, Jesus' followers waited, feeling more powerless, more hopeless, than they had ever felt in their lives.

For all that time, hope is dead. For more than twenty-four un-explainable hours, the Son of God, the hope of the world, simply lies there in a tomb.

And what about his close friends? What about his disciples? They are as dead inside as the master they had watched die. Their sense of helplessness and hopelessness all but overwhelms them.

This is what we often see in Plan B circumstances. An event takes place that sucks the life out of us. It drains our energy, destroys our initiative, wrecks our belief that life makes sense or that God is in control.

We are left standing, waiting, paralyzed by hopelessness. We start to wonder what the disciples must have wondered:

- Did God forget his promises?
- Does God know?
- Does God care?
- And even if he does care, does he really have the power to work this out?

There's probably no avoiding those feelings at times. But we make a big mistake if we let ourselves believe those feelings have any-thing to do with reality—because those feelings of hopelessness and helplessness usually tell us a lot more about ourselves than they do about God.

Who Drifted?

Our church was less than two years old when I received the panicked phone call that one of the teenagers in our student ministry had been involved in a life-threatening car accident. It was a Sunday evening, and I was exhausted, but I immediately took off for the emergency room at Vanderbilt Medical Center to be with the family.

I learned the family minivan had been hit in an intersection. Thirteen-year-old Chris had just taken his seatbelt off to reach a game that was on the floorboard. The impact launched him through a window, and he landed some fifty feet away. While nobody else in the accident was injured, it was immediately clear Chris had incurred life-threatening injuries.

That was a long evening as doctors fought to keep Chris alive. I remember standing with his parents beside his bed in the middle of the night, pleading with God for his life.

Chris survived that night but still had a very long road ahead of him. After several weeks, he was transferred to a hospital in Atlanta. His future was still very much up in the air. I had the opportunity to spend some time in Atlanta with his mother, Pat. We sat there talking next to Chris's bed, where he still lay in a coma after two months.

At one point, I turned to her and asked, "Pat, do you ever wonder where God is in all of this?"

She sat there for a second and then answered, "No, I really don't. I don't even ask that question. The question I ask is, where am I? God's been here with me the whole time. If I feel distant from him, it's not because he's left. It's because I've drifted."

I remember driving back to Nashville that evening and replaying Pat's words over and over in my mind. How many times had I totally missed God because I assumed he wasn't there? How many times had I missed an opportunity to know him on a more intimate level but missed him because I had drifted in the midst of the crisis, in the midst of the waiting? How many times have I missed seeing him work because I got bogged down in my helplessness and allowed myself to lose hope?

Can I say something about those times when life seems to be out of control? Let's use the disciples as an example. Their dream seems to be dead. Nothing seems to be happening. They feel hopeless, as if they're all alone.

But wouldn't you agree that, as they walk away from the cross that day, God is actually doing his best work yet?

Now, the last thing I want to do is plant false hope inside of you while you're grappling with a messed-up, out-of-control Plan B. The last thing I want to do is propose a simplistic solution to a problem that is far from simple.

But I've walked enough people through enough Plan Bs to ask in all seriousness: Is it possible God is getting ready to do a work in you? Is it possible that God is preparing to take your impossible situation and turn it around? I'm not saying he is, but is it possible?

Hang on to that while we look at what happened next with Jesus' helpless, hopeless disciples.

Saturday

It was Friday, remember, when Jesus was crucified. But the paralyzing hopelessness the disciples experience continues to intensify as they move into Saturday.

I think it's interesting that we don't talk a lot about Saturday. We spend a lot of time talking about Good Friday, which of course we should. This is the day redemption happened through the shedding of Christ's blood. It's a very important day.

Nobody would argue Easter Sunday is a day of celebration. We celebrate that Jesus conquered death so we can have life. It doesn't get any better than Easter Sunday.

But we don't hear a lot about Saturday, do we? Saturday seems like a day when nothing is happening. It's a day of questioning, doubting, wondering, and definitely waiting. It's the day of helplessness and hopelessness. It's a day when we begin to wonder if God is asleep at the wheel or simply powerless to do anything about our problems.

Is it possible, though, that Saturday is actually a day of preparation? Is it possible God's getting ready to do his best work in us?

That's exactly what was happening on that Saturday after Jesus' crucifixion. Saturday was the day God was engineering a resurrection:

> Very early on the first day of the week, at dawn, the women came to the tomb, bringing the spices they had prepared. They found the stone rolled away from the entrance of the tomb, but when they went in, they did not find the body of the Lord Jesus. While they were wondering about this, two men in shining clothes suddenly stood beside them. The women were very afraid and bowed their heads to the ground. The men said to them, "Why are you looking for a living person in this place for the dead? He is not here; he has risen from the dead. Do you remember what he told you in Galilee? He said the Son of Man must be handed over to sinful people, be crucified, and rise from the dead on the third day." (Luke 24:1–7)

You may currently be in the midst of a horrible, out-of-control situation. You feel as if God is not there, that there's nothing that can be done.

But here is the message of the gospel for you while you're stuck in your helpless, hopeless Saturday life: God does his best work in hopeless situations.

We worship a God who specializes in resurrections. He specializes in hopeless situations. After all, he conquered death—the ultimate hopeless situation—so you could have life.

His followers were dejected and dismal and hopeless, and then Jesus rose from the dead. God did the impossible, and in a matter of hours, the disciples journeyed from hopeless to hope-filled. From powerless to powerful. They saw him risen, and everything changed. There was this unstoppable force of hope in them that allowed them to go on to help change the world.

And you may say, "Well, good for them."

Nope.

Good for us. Good for me. Good for you. Good for anyone who is in desperate need of hope today.

Here is the message of the gospel for you while
you're stuck in your helpless, hopeless Saturday life:
God does his best work in hopeless situations.

You see, the resurrection is more than just a historical reality. We don't gather on Easter weekend all around the world just to celebrate a moment in history. We gather together to remind each other that what happened two thousand years ago changed this world forever. It changed my life forever. It can change yours as well, if you let it.

You see, there are two very different types of hope in this world. One is hoping for something, and the other is hoping in someone.

One day, everything we hope for will eventually disappoint us. Every circumstance, every situation, every relationship we put our hope in is going to wear out, give out, fall apart, melt down, and go away.

That's the problem with hoping in something. That's why the only dependable hope is hope in someone. Or rather, Someone. The entirety of Scripture points to one cross, one man, one God—not because he gives us everything we're hoping for but because he is the One in whom we put our hope.

This is why I can have hope in the midst of my crisis. I can have hope when there is no circumstantial reason to have hope. My hope is not based on what the stock market does or what others think of me or whether my life turns out the way I want it to turn out.

My hope is based on a powerful, in-control God who can do and will do the impossible.

My hope is based on a God who has defeated death itself.

The Same Power

And here's something else that God promises. Just allow the words of Ephesians 1:19–20 to sink in.

> You will know that God's power is very great for us who believe.
> That power is the same as the great strength God used to raise Christ
> from the dead and put him at his right side in the heavenly world.

Read that one more time. Did you get it? *The same power* that was at work in Christ is now at work in us.

Who? All of us? No, not all of us. In those "who believe."

Because listen—most people just don't go there. Most people want to believe in a lot of other things that might give them hope. They want to trust the market to pull them out of a financial crisis. They want to trust a counselor to help them turn around a dead-end marriage. They want to trust themselves to figure a way out of their Plan B situations.

They don't want to believe that they're really helpless and hopeless.

But this is a very important point. The reason Plan B tends to make us feel so helpless and hopeless is that, apart from the power of Christ, we really are!

We may have gifts and talents. We may have outstanding abilities and impressive energies. We might have willpower and persever-ance . . . up to a point. But as our Plan Bs show all too clear, we're far more limited than we like to admit.

We don't have the power to transform our lives.

We can't manufacture hope. None of us can.

We don't possess the antidote to our lust, our anger, our bitter-ness, our laziness, and all that poison that has been contaminating us for years. No matter how much we want to, we're not going to be able to fix ourselves.

We certainly don't have the power to raise to life that which is dead! We can't resurrect anything.

But Christ can. And the power of Christ is available to us and in us who believe.

I think this verse in Ephesians may be one of the best kept secrets in the church today!

The other day I was walking around the house looking for my keys. I'm embarrassed at how often I lose those shiny things. I was late for a meeting, and I was tearing the house apart looking for them. (I've discovered you never lose your keys when you're not in a hurry. It's a scientific fact.)

I started to pray, *God, please help me find my keys. I'm gonna cuss if I don't find these dang keys.* At this point I'm on about my fourth pass through the house and I'm starting to sweat. Where are my keys?!

Then Brandi says, "Well, where did you put them last?" While marital wisdom is not the point of this book, please allow me to offer a helpful tidbit. When your spouse has lost something and is feverishly looking for the lost item, please do not ask him where he put it last. If he knew where he put it, he would go there and pick it up.

Anyway, during my fifth pass through the house, Brandi calmly says, "Have you checked your pocket?" I reach down to feel the pocket of my jeans. And sure enough, my keys were right in my pocket. (Go ahead and laugh now. I'm over it.)

Listen, the Bible tells us that God's power is available to us, so why are we walking around all lost looking for it? It's right there.

In me? Yes.

The power of Christ is in you who believe.

You have a power available to you. You have a hope available to you. When Christ rose from the dead, he was communicating to every one of us who call ourselves believers that we, too, can rise above the hopelessness of the moment we feel trapped in.

Yes, even our out-of-control, Plan B circumstances.

Come to Me

Today I want you to know—and this is all that matters—Christ was crucified for the redemption of sins. He was buried in the ground because he was dead. God the Father brought him back to life. And that very same power is available to those who believe.

I don't know what in your life appears dead. I don't know what appears to be in the tomb for you.

I don't care if it's your marriage, your career, your finances, your health, or your dreams. I don't care what's in the tomb. I don't care if it seems like it's been in the tomb for days like Jesus was . . . or for two months . . . or six years. When Jesus Christ shows up at your tomb, he can set you free. He can breathe life into you.

Maybe you're reading this and realize you have never put your ultimate hope in Jesus Christ. You can do that right now. Confess your sin and ask forgiveness. Receive life. Put your life and your eternal destiny in his hands. And when you do that, you have put your hope in the one place on earth where no power can touch it—no circumstance, no disappointment, no accident, no guilt, no regret, no mistake. Not even death itself.

While life is uncertain, God is not.
While our power is limited, God's is limitless.
While our hope may be fragile, God is hope himself.

And no, that doesn't take away your cancer.

That doesn't erase the bankruptcy you're in the midst of.

That doesn't heal your broken relationship.

That doesn't replace your shattered dream.

But it can remind you that while life is uncertain, God is not. While our power is limited, God's is limitless. He still has the whole world in his hands. While our hope may be fragile, God is hope himself.

Your world may feel chaotic, especially when you're stuck in a Saturday, struggling hopelessly with your Plan B.

But no doubt about it, God is still in control. And one way or another, Sunday is about to dawn.

TWELVE WAITING ON GOD

I met Todd and Angie Smith several years ago through some mutual friends. Todd is in a Christian group called Selah and has experienced tremendous success in his career. He has one of the most incredible voices I've ever heard.

Todd and Angie are one of those couples Brandi and I just hit it off with from the first time we met them. They're just salt-of-the-earth kind of people. It also helps that they have three beautiful girls around the same ages as our boys . . . and the boys are totally enamored with them.

We were so excited when Todd and Angie found out last year they were pregnant with number four. I suspected Todd was secretly hoping for a boy this time. But in truth, as always, we were all just praying for a healthy baby.

Around the sixteen-week mark in the pregnancy, Todd's dreams of having his first boy were dashed. An ultrasound confirmed he and Angie were having yet another baby girl. Todd and Angie were in the thick of preparing the baby's room, making plans, and generally getting excited about their new addition, whom they named Audrey, when they received a disturbing phone call.

At week eighteen, a nurse called to say some abnormalities in an early test indicated baby Audrey might have Down syndrome. They would have to wait a couple of weeks to do further testing, but Todd and Angie began trying to adjust to this possibility. Angie remembers, "Over the next couple of weeks we just prayed and prayed, and we finally got to a place where we were settled with having a special-needs child. We were peaceful and felt equipped."

But the next ultrasound, at twenty weeks, revealed that the problems with Audrey were more complicated than originally thought. Todd says, "We could tell just looking at the doctor's face as he read the ultrasound that something was terribly wrong. He then rambled on about her condition. The only word I heard him say was *fatal*."

Angie recalls, "All I remember about that day was laying my head on Todd's shoulder and saying, 'Is this really happening?' We went into the doctor's office praying Audrey was not going to have Down syndrome, and we walked out wishing that was all she had."

Todd and Angie left the doctor's office that day feeling shocked and overwhelmed. They were told they should terminate their pregnancy because the baby would never survive outside the womb. At best, she would take a few breaths before dying.

As you can imagine, the next few months were an emotional roller coaster for the Smiths. Angie said they were trying to find a "balance between planning for loss and hoping for miracles."

I think that statement describes what so many of us feel in the midst of a Plan B. We want to believe somehow God can and will redeem our Plan B mess, but we're just not sure how anything good could come out of this particular situation. We want to hope, but hope seems distant and far-fetched and maybe even inappropriate.

Have you ever felt that way? Do you feel that way now?

Well, I can't tell you with any confidence that everything will turn out a particular way for you. I can't tell you when your Plan B will settle down and resolve itself. I can't even tell you things will get better. I just don't have that information. No one does.

But I can tell you that God has a perspective on life we don't have—and God is working in your situation right now, even if you can't see it.

If you had been at the cross on the day Christ was crucified, you would have sworn that was the worst thing that could ever happen. We don't see it that way today, do we? We have a couple thousand years of perspective, and now many of us perceive the cross as the most beautiful thing we have seen in our lives.

We think that because it reminds us that God can take the worst things and turn them into something good.

After all, he's already taken the worst event in history and turned it into the best thing that ever happened to us.

And that's a reason to keep hoping even when we must watch and wait.

Searching for True Hope

I need to point out something about hope here because hope can be kind of tricky. It can be directed toward what is objectively bad and still be hope. You can hope for bad things to happen. You can also hope for things that aren't worth hoping for, things that aren't good for you. You can waste energy hoping for something that has no chance of happening.

St. Augustine said, "There are two things that kill the soul: despair and false hope." With that in mind we must be very careful when it comes to hope.

Dr. Lewis Smedes explains:

Hope, like love, can be fake. And when it is, we pay heavily for counting on it. A hope may be false because it is based on other people's lies. But it can also be false because we falsify it ourselves. We can use hope as a cheap escape from the messes we create. We turn hope false by expecting a happiness that the thing we hope for cannot bring. We turn hope false when we hope out of mean spirit. And we turn hope false when we hope to overcome pain before we can even feel it.[1]

Now, while some would argue with me, I would say hope has been implanted in us as a natural inclination in the same way faith and love have. We're born with the desire to see new possibilities, to long for something better than what we see at the moment. Hope is just built into our being.

"Then why don't I feel hopeful?" you may say. "Why do I feel despair?"

I think your hope is still there, but you've fallen for the fallacy of false hope. As we saw in the last chapter, you may have been hoping *for something* instead of hoping *in someone*. Hoping for something will almost always disappoint. Hoping in God will always move toward something good, even if we can't see it.

It's in that vein that the book of James urges us . . .

My brothers and sisters, when you have many kinds of troubles, you should be full of joy, because you know that these troubles test your faith, and this will give you patience. Let your patience show itself perfectly in what you do. Then you will be perfect and complete and will have everything you need. (James 1:2–4)

"You should be full of joy," James tells us. Be full of joy when you face difficult times. Be full of joy when a dream dissipates or a desire is crushed. And why? Because you're about to be freed from a false hope and redirected toward a true hope.

That's what our Plan B difficulties can do for us if we let them. That's what our painful times of waiting for God to act can do. They can deliver us from our delusions, our misguided expectations, our egotistical dreams, and deliver us into the actual presence of the God who is our only true hope. They can teach us the patience and trust to let God change us the way he needs to change us.

I would say I've never met someone who has an authentically intimate relationship with God who doesn't have a story about this. A story about facing what seemed to be a hopeless situation and emerging on the other side, not necessarily with the hoped-for outcome, but with something precious and new—a fresh awareness and intimacy with God.

There is an undeniable relationship between crisis
and hope. Between waiting hopefully and being
transformed. Between Plan B and the glory of God.

Perhaps it has happened to you in an earlier Plan B experience. You had to go through something you didn't expect. A pivotal, defining moment when it felt as if God was a long way away.

This was the moment the Bible became more than just stories. It became personal.

This was the moment God became more than just a cosmic being, when he became "Father God."

This was the moment church became more than just a place you attend on Sunday. It became a community of support.

If that hasn't happened to you yet, I hope you will let it happen— because it can. I've seen it over and over. I've had it happen to me.

One of the things I want to help you see is there is an undeniable relationship between crisis and hope. Between waiting hopefully and being transformed. Between Plan B and the glory of God.

And this is important: the hope, the transformation, the glory doesn't necessarily happen on Sunday when the crisis is over and the Saturday waiting is done and Plan B is just a memory.

The hope and transformation and glory is part of the whole process—as we see in the biblical story of Lazarus, his sisters, and their good friend Jesus.

The Glory Plan

This story, which is told in John 11, begins in the town of Bethany, where Lazarus lives with his sisters, Mary and Martha. Jesus is well acquainted with this family. In fact, they are dear friends, and their house has long been a home away from home for him and his disciples.

Jesus is far away from Bethany when the story begins. He has traveled "across the Jordan River" (John 10:40) to get away from religious authorities who are trying to arrest him. But while Jesus is doing his work across the Jordan, he gets bad news from Bethany. Here's how the Bible tells the story:

> Now a man named Lazarus was sick . . . So the sisters sent word to Jesus, "Lord, the one you love is sick." When he heard this, Jesus said, "This sickness will not end in death. No, it is for God's glory so that God's Son may be glorified through it." Jesus loved Martha and her sister and Lazarus. Yet when he heard that Lazarus was sick, he stayed where he was two more days. (John 11:1–6 NIV)

This seems like a shocking response to this sad Plan B situation. Jesus not only seems strangely unconcerned about his friend's illness and the family's worry and fear but also says it has a purpose, that it's actually for God's glory.

But that can be hard to take, especially when we're slogging our way through the pain and frustration of a Plan B. It's hard to think we have to go through all that just so God can be glorified.

I heard a pastor once referring to this passage say, "I don't like that glory plan."

I have to agree with him. I mean, I want to give God glory, I just want to do it in a different way. Right?

I like the glory plan where I throw the winning touchdown pass and then I point up at the sky as I run off the field.

I like the glory plan where I win an Oscar and then say, "I just want to give God all the glory."

I like the glory plan where I write a best-selling book, and then I say, "It wasn't me—it was all God."

We don't like God's glory plan—
not if it involves *our* suffering.
Not if it involves waiting for God and wondering if
he's ever going to act. Not if it involves Plan B.

I don't want the plan where a dream is crushed, a crisis is experienced, or I feel like I'm walking alone for way too long . . . and then God gets the glory.

I think Francis Chan got right to the heart of the matter when he wrote the following:

> You passionately love Jesus, but you don't really want to be like Him. You admire His humility, but you don't want to be *that* humble. You think it's beautiful that He washed the feet of the disciples, but that's not exactly the direction your life is headed. You're thankful He was spit upon and abused, but you would never let that happen to you. You praise Him for loving you enough to suffer during His whole time on earth, but you're going to do everything within your power to make sure you enjoy your time down here.
>
> In short: You think He is a great Savior, but not a great role model.[2]

I suspect that's how most of us feel, if we're really honest. We don't like God's glory plan—not if it involves *our* suffering. Not if it involves waiting for God and wondering if he's ever going to act. Not if it involves Plan B. We love the idea of following Jesus until it disrupts our plans and dreams.

When I read John 11, I'm pretty sure that Mary and Martha and Lazarus weren't too fond of God's glory plan either—not when they were right in the middle of waiting for Jesus to show up.

No Answer

Can you imagine what it was like for that little family at Bethany after handing the messenger the note about Lazarus being ill?

Picture Lazarus in his bed, burning with fever, growing sicker and sicker. Mary sits by his side, crying, holding his hand. Martha bustles about, managing the sickroom efficiently but unable to hide her worry. All of them are thinking, *Jesus will be here any minute. Jesus can help. Should we send another messenger? C'mon, Jesus . . .*

But Jesus doesn't come.

You've felt that frustration in your life, haven't you! *God, I need you to help me. I promise I'll start reading the Bible again. I promise I won't drift away from you again. I'll be a missionary or whatever. Just help me.*

And nothing.

Nothing changes. Nothing gets better. If God is doing anything, you can't tell.

It's like you take the same dang prayer request to your small group or Sunday school class every week. Even they are tired of hearing about it. They write your request down before they even get to you.

And still you wait. And nothing seems to change.

The Waiting Game

Don't you hate waiting? Most of us do. Waiting has never been a popular pastime, and our culture makes it worse. We live in the day of fast this and instant that, and having to wait is a big frustration. We've started to believe faster is always better. We've become seduced by such words as *instant* and *easy*. We've become quickaholics—dependent on getting what we want when we want it.

I must confess that's true of me too. I don't like standing in line at the bank or post office, and I sure don't like waiting in traffic. And if I can just be honest with you, I really hate waiting on God.

Why do we hate waiting so much? There are many reasons, but I think one of the biggest is that waiting makes us feel powerless. Or rather, waiting reminds us just how powerless we really are. Lewis Smedes describes it like this:

> Waiting is our destiny. As creatures who cannot by themselves bring about what they hope for, we wait in the darkness for a flame we cannot light. We wait in fear for a happy ending that we cannot write. We wait for a "not yet" that feels like a "not ever."[3]

Throughout the first part of our Lazarus story, Mary and Martha learn a lot about that awful, endless, hopeless feeling that comes from waiting. For days they stand out at the road waiting and waiting for Jesus to show up. They just know he can heal Lazarus. But has anyone seen Jesus?

They watch, and they wait. And while Jesus is taking his precious time, they slowly watch their brother die.

We've started to believe faster is always better.
We've become seduced by such words as *instant*
and *easy*. We've become quickaholics—dependent
on getting what we want when we want it.

The Whys of Waiting

Every two weeks after Todd and Angie were told baby Audrey's condition was fatal, they returned to the hospital for an ultrasound. Some weeks it seemed as if God was healing Audrey. Other weeks it was clear her little organs were continuing to deteriorate. The jolt from hope to despair was unlike anything they had ever experienced.

One day, Angie told me later, she just drove and drove around Nashville screaming at God. "God, why won't you heal my baby? Why won't you do this? Why does this have to be us? Why, God? Why?"

Then, just weeks before Audrey's scheduled birth, Angie found herself in a situation that wrecks me every time I think about it. She and Todd were continuing to wait and pray and hope for a miracle, but they were also preparing for the worst. So she visited the cemetery to pick a spot and headstone for her unborn baby. Angie wrote on her blog that day, "No mother should have to walk around and look at tombstones for her baby while that baby hiccups and shifts within her."

Can we be honest for a second? Isn't it difficult to wait on God when you feel like he's abandoned you? Don't you find it difficult to be faithful to God when you don't feel like he has been faithful to you?

Can I point out that Todd and Angie and Mary and Martha were not the first people left waiting on God to act? The Bible is full of people who spend months or years or even decades waiting:

- Abraham and Sarah waited expectantly to have a child (Gen. 11–21).
- Jacob waited (and worked) for Rachel to be his wife (Gen. 28–29).
- Joseph waited longingly in prison (Gen. 30:20–41:39).
- John the Baptist also waited to be rescued from prison (John 14:1–12).
- Noah waits a hundred and fifty days for the floodwaters to recede (Gen. 6–7).
- The Israelites waited some forty years to enter the promised land.
- The early Christians waited for Jesus to return.

Some of these biblical people eventually saw their hopes fulfilled. Some eventually were able to stop waiting and finally celebrate what they'd waited for. But not everyone. And not completely, as Hebrews 11:13 reminds us: "All these great people died in faith. They did not get the things that God promised his people, but they saw them coming far in the future and were glad. They said they were like visitors and strangers on earth."

Even Jesus had a time of waiting, as Henri Nouwen explains:

The central word in the story of Jesus' arrest is one I never thought much about. It is "to be handed over." Judas handed Jesus over . . . The remarkable thing is that the same word is used not only for Judas but also for God. God did not spare Jesus, but handed him over to benefit us all (see Romans 8:32). So this word, "to be handed over," plays a central role in the life of Jesus. Indeed, this drama of being handed over divides the life of Jesus radically in two.[4]

Nouwen goes on to point out that Jesus spends the first part of his life in activity—teaching, traveling, taking initiative, healing people, and doing things. But after he's handed over, "he becomes the one to whom things are being done."[5] He is now not doing, but waiting. And it's in this waiting that he lives out his deepest and truest purpose.

But what is the purpose of Mary and Martha's waiting? It's still not entirely clear as the story continues:

Then Jesus said to his followers, "Let's go back to Judea."

The followers said, "But Teacher, some people there tried to stone you to death only a short time ago. Now you want to go back there?"

Jesus answered, "Are there not twelve hours in the day? If anyone walks in the daylight, he will not stumble, because he can see by this world's light. But if anyone walks at night, he stumbles because there is no light to help him see."

After Jesus said this, he added, "Our friend Lazarus has fallen asleep, but I am going there to wake him."

The followers said, "But Lord, if he is only asleep, he will be all right."

Jesus meant that Lazarus was dead, but his followers thought he meant Lazarus was really sleeping. [Ever wonder if Jesus under his breath whispered, "God, these guys are killing me"?] So then Jesus said plainly, "Lazarus is dead. And I am glad for your sakes I was not there so that you may believe. But let's go to him now." (vv. 7–15)

What?

Time out! What did Jesus just say? Did he just say he's glad he wasn't there for his good friend's death? That he's happy not to be there to support his good friends Mary and Martha? That he's gratified he's been absent while they waited and waited for something good to happen?

Yes, that's exactly what he said.

And why in the world would he say something like that?

According the Scriptures, "so that you may believe." So the disciples (and our) faith in him might be strengthened and our hope in God will be renewed.

That was the purpose (or part of it) in all that waiting.

Am I saying God sends these trials, these hopeless situations into our lives, into the lives of people like Todd and Angie, just so we'll get our hope realigned with him?

No, I'm not saying that at all.

But I am saying God will absolutely *allow* suffering, pain, and crisis in order to detach hope from other things and attach it to himself. He will *use* the suffering of Plan B to strengthen our faith.

That is, if we will let him. If we will trust him and let him work.

You've got to stop looking at your shattered dreams and your unmet expectations as something God is doing to you. He's not doing something to you. But he might be doing something *through* you. He might be doing something *in* you.

Just as he was doing for Mary and Martha and Lazarus and the disciples.

And just as he was doing for those who gathered for Lazarus's funeral.

A Question of Timing

When Jesus arrived, he learned that Lazarus had already been dead and in the tomb for four days. Bethany was about two miles from Jerusalem. Many of the Jews had come there to comfort Martha and Mary about their brother.

When Martha heard that Jesus was coming, she went out to meet him, but Mary stayed home. Martha said to Jesus, "Lord, if you had been here, my brother would not have died." (vv. 17–21)

You've probably said this too. "God, if you had been here, this wouldn't have happened. God, where were you?"

I know you could have saved my marriage.

I know you could have gotten me that promotion.

I know you could have healed my child.

I know you can make us pregnant today if you want to.

I know you could've done something.

Where were you?

Notice in this passage Mary is not doubting God's power. She's questioning his timing. She's ticked off because he didn't show up when she wanted him to show up.

That's worth noting because I believe often that's our issue too.

The question isn't *can you trust God?* Of course you can trust God.

The question is *can you wait?* Will you wait? Will you continue to hope in him even when his timing seems all off?

Angie discovered in the midst of their crisis an entirely new reality of trust. She says, "Growing up, I was blessed to have a father whom I could always trust. If my dad said he was going to be there at nine forty-five, he would be there at nine thirty. Trust meant it was going to happen the way I anticipated it was going to happen. God's showing me these days that's not necessarily what trust is. Trust is believing someone is going to be with you no matter what the road is doing in front of you or behind you."

In other words, trusting in God does not mean God shows up for you exactly the way you thought he was going to show up. Trusting God doesn't mean his timing is going to be your timing.

Going for Transformation

Hope does not come only from believing God's power, but also from accepting and trusting his timing. And that's hard to do. We want his power. We want his comfort. But often we don't want his calendar. We want him to show up when we want him, in the way we want.

Mark Batterson wrote the following in *Wild Goose Chase*:

I tend to live the way I drive. I want to get from point A to point B in the shortest amount of time and by the easiest route possible. But I've come to realize that getting where God wants me to go isn't nearly as important as becoming who God wants me to be in the process. And God seems to be far less concerned with where I'm going than with who I'm becoming.[6]

And that, I believe, is an important key to all that miserable waiting we do, waiting for God to show up and resolve our Plan B turmoil. We're interested in getting our problems solved and our lives back to normal. But what God is really interested in is who we can become. He wants us to have more faith. He wants us to have true hope. That is so important to him that he will leverage anything in our lives to help it happen.

Spiritual transformation doesn't take place on Sunday when we get what we want. It takes place on Saturday while we're waiting. It's what is forged while we're waiting, hoping, trusting, even though we have yet to receive that for which we long.

But God has made his purposes clear. He's not interested in our having "a good life." He's interested in an intimate relationship with us. He's interested in our spiritual transformation.

And here's the thing about spiritual transformation (which we'll look at in more depth in the next chapter). Spiritual transformation doesn't take place on Sunday when we get what we want. It takes place on Saturday while we're waiting. It's what is forged while we're waiting, hoping, trusting, even though we have yet to receive that for which we long.

Sue Monk Kidd said it like this:

Transformations come only as we go the long way round, only as we're willing to walk a different, longer, more arduous, more inward, more prayerful route. When you wait, you're deliberately choosing to take the long way, to go eight blocks instead of four, trusting that there's a transforming discovery lying pooled along the way.[7]

In Him

Martha, as difficult as her waiting must be, shows exactly that kind of trust when she meets Jesus on the road. Within a breath of asking him where he's been, she makes this powerful statement of faith: "But I know that even now God will give you whatever you ask" (v. 22).

"Even though you haven't acted in the way I expected," she's saying, "you're still God. You're all powerful and I'm not. You're all knowing and I'm not. You're God and I'm not." She's showing the trust that is the key to spiritual transformation.

In a sense, Martha's statement of faith is a more surprising and potent miracle than what comes next. And if you know this story, you know the upcoming miracle is a doozy:

> Jesus . . . cried out in a loud voice, "Lazarus, come out!" The dead man came out, his hands and feet wrapped with pieces of cloth, and a cloth around his face. Jesus said to them, "Take the cloth off of him and let him go." Many of the people, who had come to visit Mary and saw what Jesus did, believed in him. (vv. 43–45)

You see, Jesus does end up resurrecting Lazarus from the dead. But in the process he also fulfills his purposes—to help people believe, and to bring God glory, both there at the tomb and in the lives of these people whom he loves.

It's a powerful story reminding us we should never give up hoping. We worship a God who specializes in resurrections. He specializes in hopeless situations.

That may not answer the questions you're asking—your whys and whens and hows and wheres. I don't know the answers to those questions. I don't know why you're having to wait to hear from God. I don't know why your prayers don't seem to be answered.

But I do know this: when life isn't turning out the way you had hoped, when it's Saturday and you're waiting and longing, when you feel alone and abandoned . . . God wants you to find your hope in him.

Two Hours

On April 7, 2008, Audrey Caroline Smith was born. Todd had the opportunity to hold her first, but he quickly laid the sweet baby beside Angie. Angie remembers, "To see her was to fall in love with her. She looked just like our other girls. She was so beautiful. I put my hands on her head and pulled her close so I could smell her. God let us see her alive. It was so amazing."

Todd adds, "We just kept telling her how much we loved her, and how beautiful she was. We just took her in."

"The nurse kept coming in and checking her heartbeat, and it kept getting slower and slower. But even in that moment we felt as if God could perform a miracle," Angie says. "I just kept praying 'It's not too late, God. It's not too late.'"

Sadly, two and a half hours after being born, Audrey Caroline went to be with her Creator. But to Todd and Angie, even the timing of her death was a gift.

"We were expecting two minutes," Todd says, "and God gave us two and a half hours. I wouldn't trade those two hours for anything."

I think Angie summed it up well when she wrote to Audrey in her journal, "You weighed three pounds, but your life mattered. You can go through all the reasons of why, but he allowed it to happen so he could draw people to himself. We feel we were chosen to be a part of this."

It's so important to realize waiting does not always lead to the outcome we hoped for. But you already know this. That's part of what makes waiting so difficult.

If you're in the midst of waiting for a miracle or waiting for a dream to be realized, you probably feel helpless. You may feel frustrated and grumpy or just plain old tired of waiting. You may feel like the waiting is a waste of time as if you're doing nothing.

But you're not doing nothing, not at all.

In fact, this waiting may be the most important something you can and need to do.

What you're doing is allowing your hope to grow up. And if you can't be still and wait and hope, even when you have no reason to hope, you can't become the person God created when he thought you into existence.

So no matter how it may seem, how frustrating and painful and pointless it may seem, your waiting does have a purpose. Sue Monk Kidd reminds us:

> Waiting is the in-between time. It calls us to be in this moment, this season, without leaning so far into the future that we tear our roots from the present. When we learn to wait, we experience where we are as what is truly substantial and precious in life.[8]

While You Wait . . . Rest

It's still not easy, though, is it? We still have to cope with all that restlessness and worry, those feelings of helplessness and frustration. How can you live while you're waiting for God to show up in your Plan B circumstance? How can you handle your Saturday feelings?

I have to believe God knows our periods of waiting will be quite difficult for most of us. Maybe that's why over and over again Scripture reminds us of the importance of leaning on him in trust even while we're waiting for something to work out with our Plan Bs. For instance:

> *Wait for the LORD's help.*
> *Be strong and brave,*
> *and wait for the LORD's help. (Ps. 27:14)*

> *I wait for the Lord to help me,*
> *and I trust his word. (Ps. 130:5)*

> *I find rest in God;*
> *only he gives me hope.*
> *He is my rock and my salvation.*
> *He is my defender;*
> *I will not be defeated. (Ps. 62:5–6)*

I love the word picture that comes to my mind when I read that last passage. I picture myself frustrated, angry, tired, stressed, confused, and exhausted, simply collapsing in the arms of my heavenly Father.

You may need to do just that too. Just collapse in his arms and allow him to fill you with his comfort.

Relax and allow him to be your rock and fortress during this uncertain time.

Rest in him while you're waiting, and let him be your hope.

THIRTEEN

TRANSFORMATION THROUGH TRAGEDY

Do you want to know the greatest fear I have for you—and, if I'm honest, the greatest fear I have for myself?

It isn't that we'll abandon the gospel. It's not that we'll lose complete faith in our Savior. It's not that we'll go crazy and abandon our morals.

No, my greatest fear for my life and for yours is that we'll just get busy and distracted and settle for a mediocre, unexamined life. It's that we'll just settle into life as usual and never become the persons God intended for us to be.

And here's something I've been wondering as I studied and prayed about this book. Could it be that we *need* our Plan B situations to rescue us from that kind of life?

Do we *need* our tragedies in order for God to transform us?

Well, it might be pushing things to say our tragedies are necessary for transformation. But it's true that God tends to get our attention through our Plan B crises. In fact, many of us started our journey with God during such a difficult time. And I know that when I'm struggling with a Plan B situation, I tend to pray more, read more scriptures, and lean into community a lot harder.

I also tend to experience a deeper level of intimacy with God when going through a crisis. I hate this about myself, but it's true. When things are going my way, I tend to become quite self-reliant and *very* busy. I become absorbed in my agenda for my life and may even fall into using people to get what I think I want.

I'm pretty sure I'm not the only one who does that. Henri Nouwen observes:

> One of the most obvious characteristics of our daily lives is that we are busy. We experience our days as filled with things to do, people to meet, projects to finish, letters to write, calls to make, and appointments to keep. Our lives often seem like over-packed suitcases bursting at the seams. In fact, we are almost always aware of being behind schedule. There is a nagging sense that there are unfinished tasks, unfulfilled promises, and unrealized proposals. There is always something else that we should have remembered, done, or said. There are always people we did not speak to, write to, or visit. Thus, although we are very busy, we have lingering feelings of never really fulfilling our obligations . . . Beneath our worrying lives, however, something else is going on. While our minds and hearts are filled with many things, and we wonder how we can live up to the expectations imposed upon us by ourselves and others, we have a deep sense of unfulfillment. While busy with and worried about many things, we seldom feel truly satisfied, at peace, at home. A gnawing sense of being unfilled underlies our filled lives . . . The great paradox of our time is that many of us are busy and bored at the same time.
>
> While running from one event to the next, we wonder in our innermost selves if anything is really happening. While we can hardly keep up with our many tasks and obligations, we are not so sure that it would make any difference if we did nothing at all. While people keep pushing us in all directions, we doubt if anyone really cares. In short, while our lives are full, we are unfulfilled.[1]

As much as I hate Plan Bs, nothing—and I repeat, nothing—causes me to pause from the busyness of life and examine myself like a crisis.

So maybe it's fair to say that while God doesn't *need* our tragedies to transform us, he certainly uses our Plan Bs to bring about change in our lives.

My greatest fear for my life and for yours is that we'll just get busy and distracted and settle for a mediocre, unexamined life. It's that we'll just settle into life as usual and never become the persons God intended for us to be.

The Megaphone of Pain

C. S. Lewis is famous for saying, "God whispers to us in our pleasures, speaks to us in our conscience, but shouts in our pains: It is his megaphone to rouse a deaf world."[2]

It certainly was the megaphone that roused the Davis family. Justin and Trisha Davis, along with their three boys, have been friends of mine for almost nine years. Justin and I had the opportunity to serve together on a church staff until he felt called to start a church in the Indianapolis area. He launched Genesis Church, and it was an overnight success. They were reaching hundreds of people, and the church was growing like crazy.

However, unknown to anyone, Justin was battling a longstanding sexual addiction. Even as his church grew, he was slipping deeper and deeper into a fantasy world of pornography, with all kinds of ramifications. His marriage deteriorated, and he continued to make unwise choices.

Then on October 9, 2005, the bomb dropped. Justin sat down

with Trisha to tell her he was having an affair with her best friend, who was also the children's director at the church.

In that moment they both felt as if this was a crisis and tragedy they would never rebound from. It was lights out. The dream was over. They had no other options but to separate and walk away. Everything they cared about—the church, their family, their friends— was in jeopardy.

You may not have had a choice on whether you could
have kids or whether your loved one passed away
or whether you got fired or your husband had an affair.
But you do get to choose how you respond.
And in that choice lies an amazing amount of hope.

I've noticed before that people often don't feel like they have any choices when they're going through a Plan B. They feel as if all of their options have been taken away. And that's true to a certain extent—but only to a certain extent.

You may not have had a choice on whether you could have kids or whether your loved one passed away or whether you got fired or your husband had an affair.

But you do get to choose how you respond.

And in that choice lies an amazing amount of hope.

That choice is what makes the journey of transformation possible.

The Journey

It seems to me more and more Christians I know today have abandoned the faith because they simply could not see the transforming work God was doing in the midst of their tragedy. Their pain, their confusion, and their questions drowned out their opportunity for growth.

Several years ago, I was out in Colorado with my good friend and former college roommate Kevin Colon. While on a retreat with several other pastors, we heard a rumor that there was a hidden lake several miles up the mountain from where we were staying.

Being avid fly fishermen, we couldn't let an opportunity like that go by without exploring to see if there might be some brook trout in that lake. So Kevin and I made up our minds to hike to that lake.

We left early that morning and headed up the mountain, but the hike was much more difficult than we had imagined. We continually lost the trail and our sense of direction. At one point we saw some very large mountain lion tracks in the snow, and that was enough to convince us that maybe we should head back down the mountain. So we gave up and came back down.

I could tell several of the guys in our group were disappointed Kevin and I didn't make it to the top to find the lake. While they didn't want to hike up it, they did want to enjoy our little adventure vicariously. We were disappointed too. We had really wanted to get in some fishing. So later that afternoon, we decided to give it another try.

Our second attempt wasn't any easier than the first. We climbed and climbed and climbed. It was early spring, but the snowcaps still hadn't melted, so at times we were hiking through three-foot snowdrifts. We took several wrong turns and had to backtrack to find the path. But eventually we reached the top. And there in front of us was a beautiful, pristine lake sitting there in a little valley, surrounded by more mountains.

We spent the rest of the afternoon catching small but absolutely stunning brook trout. I wouldn't trade that experience for the world. And we almost missed it. We almost gave up not only because the journey was difficult and long, but also because our path was unclear.

I share this story because this is where you may be in your life. You're in the middle of a difficult and painful Plan B journey, and you're tempted to give up. You're tempted to turn around, but don't.

If you turn around now, you'll miss out on what God has in store for you. You'll miss out on the transformation that awaits you.

Peter Scazzero says:

> Our culture routinely interprets losses as alien invasions that interrupt our "normal" lives. We numb our pain through denial, blaming, rationalizations, addictions, and avoidance. We search for spiritual shortcuts around our wounds. We demand others take away our pain. Yet we all face many deaths within our lives. The choice is whether these deaths will be terminal (crushing our spirit and life) or open us up to new possibilities and depths of transformation in Christ.[3]

It's Not Over

Justin and Trisha Davis would be the first ones to admit their marriage had been unhealthy for years before Justin's big confession. Rationalization, blaming, and avoidance had become the norm in their home, even as they tried to pretend everything was okay.

In the days after announcing his affair to his family and church, Justin says he was overwhelmed with pain, shame, and embarrassment. He had hurt everyone he ever cared about.

"I remember a few days after everything had come out in the open, I was sitting in a little bedroom at some friends' house who were allowing me to stay with them. My friend knocked on the door and walked in carrying all my clothes and all my stuff. Trisha had packed it all up and sent it to me. When I saw all my stuff, it's like a dark cloud moved over me. He sat on the bed with me and said, 'Justin, it's going to feel like it's over, but it's not over.'"

Now, you may feel exactly like Justin did. You may be telling your-self, "It's over."

- The marriage can't be fixed.
- The friendship can't be retrieved.
- The career is ruined.
- The disease can't be cured.
- There's no way to make amends.
- It's too late to go back to school.
- It's too late to have children.
- It's too late to begin again.

So you, too, may need to hear the words of Justin's friend: It's not over. It may feel like it's over, but it's not over.

This doesn't mean that what you might want to happen is going to happen. It just means that God's not done yet. There is still time for love, grace, transformation, and redemption. It's not over.

Those words would bounce around in Justin's head for the next few days. And gradually, Justin says, "I actually started to believe, in the midst of the darkness and heartbreak and shame, that God could take this and do something. While I was devastated, I also started to feel a sense of freedom that I didn't have to hide anymore. So much had been stripped away that I could start to discover who I really am in Christ.

"It seemed discouraging and devastating and hopeless," he adds. "But I knew God still wanted to give birth to something that would not be possible had we not gone through this. I just didn't know what."

A Crisis of Transformation

I believe there is a crisis in today's church, and it's a crisis of transfor-mation. People are going to church, they're listening to the messages, they're participating in the programs, but they're not being transformed.

They're not growing in Christlikeness. The word that best describes so many Christians these days seems to be *stalled*.

I think we're all aware that there's a gap between who we are today and who God created us to be. I believe this gap will always exist this side of heaven. But here's the question we all need to be asking ourselves: "Is the gap closing? Is it narrowing, or am I stalled?"

When people become aware of the gap, they tend to do several different things. Most commonly, they try to assign blame. They blame the church, the pastors, and the programs for their lack of blame. They may even try to blame themselves.

I think we're all aware that there's a gap between who we are today and who God created us to be.
I believe this gap will always exist this side of heaven. But here's the question we all need to be asking ourselves: "Is the gap closing?
Is it narrowing, or am I stalled?"

But the reality is that blame is beside the point. The real problem is that most of us just don't understand how the gap can be narrowed. We don't understand how transformation happens. Our theology is too limited to show us how our Plan Bs can actually draw us close to our Savior and produce sustained life change.

No wonder we lose hope when we encounter a crisis.

No wonder we think it's over. (But it's not!)

The Stages of Transformation

There has actually been quite a bit of research done on the different stages we go through when it comes to spiritual transformation. In *The Critical Journey: Stages in the Life of Faith*, Janet Hagberg and Robert Guelich gather this research and develop a model that describes the different stages of faith.[4]

Stage one, according to Hagberg and Guelich, is a life-changing awareness of God. This stage comes at the beginning of our journey with Christ, as we become aware of his reality. We realize our need for mercy and grace through what Christ did on the cross and begin our relationship with him.

Hagberg and Guelich call stage two "Discipleship." This stage is characterized by learning about God and what it means to be a follower of Christ. We usually become part of a Christian community and begin to understand what it means to live a life of faith.

In stage three, which is called "The Active Life," we get actively involved in working for God, serving him and his people. We take responsibility by bringing our unique talents and gifts to serve Christ and others. This is often referred to as the "doing" stage. I might add that this is where the spiritual formation plan ends in the average American church. We tell people that they grow by doing. Serve, teach, give, and you will become more like Christ. And that, of course, is true, but it's not the complete picture. If we get stalled at this stage, we risk never quite becoming what we could be.

If we keep moving forward, though, eventually we'll hit stage four, "The Journey Inward." This is when we begin to rethink who we are and what we believe. And this inward journey may well be triggered by a Plan B situation in our lives. (Remember it's almost always a tragedy, conflict, or crisis that interrupts our busy, unexamined lives.)

Ronald Rolheiser explains what may happen when a Plan B precipitates an inward journey:

What causes the head to move from a reliance on concepts to a reliance on faith? Or the will to move from a reliance on possessions to a reliance on charity? Or the personality to move from a reliance on security and control to trusting in hope? We enter into the dark night of the spirit when we make the decision to live by raw faith . . . No longer able to derive any support from our natural faculties, we experience a horrible emptiness, a sense of weakness, a feeling of abandonment . . . the soul feels that God has rejected it and with an abhorrence of it casts it into darkness. Still, deprived of their normal way of relating to the world, our intellect, will, and memory begin to rely on faith, hope, and charity.[5]

Having questioned our faith and asked our questions, we move into stage five, "The Journey Outward." Here we may begin to do some of the same active external things we did before. But now we're operating out of a new, grounded center. We have a new sense of God's profound, deep, accepting love for us. We know now that we are not alone, regardless of what we might feel. A deep, inner stillness now begins to characterize our work for God.

And then, finally, comes stage six of the journey, "Transformed by Love." Hagberg and Guelich describe this stage as the season where God continually sends events, circumstances, people, and even books into our lives to keep us moving forward on our journey.

Now, please understand that this six-stage description of the faith journey is just a general framework, a description of how many people typically grow and change spiritually over the course of their lives if the transformative process is not blocked. The point is not to try to work your way through all six stages. The point is not that this is exactly what it's going to look like in your life. The point is for you to begin to see there is a process for spiritual transformation and that this process almost always involves a Plan B that forces you to levels of deeper intimacy with our heavenly Father.

Knowing this can give you a perspective that actually helps you be transformed through your Plan B experiences. It allows you to see your particular crisis or disappointment as a piece in the puzzle of your growth rather than as a roadblock to accomplishing your dreams. Winning and accomplishment then tend to become secondary as you begin to focus more on the process and journey God has you on.

Stripped and Purified

More than five hundred years ago, a Spanish mystic called St. John of the Cross wrote a little book called *Dark Night of the Soul*. This little book, actually a long poem with commentary, had a tremendous impact on Christians through the centuries, to the point that we routinely refer to a spiritual crisis as a "dark night of the soul." It has also had a tremendous impact on me and the way I perceive the Plan Bs in my life.

St. John of the Cross actually describes the "dark night"—I would call it Plan B—as a gift from God. And he says it involves a process of purification, letting God reveal and strip away our spiritual imperfections.

John of the Cross lists seven of these: pride, avarice, luxury, wrath, spiritual gluttony, spiritual envy, and sloth. They're old-fashioned words, but they pretty well sum up the spiritual failings that hold us back. We don't grow; we're not transformed because we're proud and arrogant, because we're greedy and want nice things more than we want God, because we hold on to anger and envy, and because we're lazy and self-indulgent.

Is a spiritual crisis the only way God rids us of such things? Absolutely not. As far as I've seen, it's a primary way he does this work of transformation in us and through us.

That was certainly true for my friend Justin. As he began to "journey inward" through his "dark night of the soul," he began to look at himself and realize he had lived most his life relying on his talent and charm. He says, "I was gifted, smooth, and wise beyond my years, but I was operating out of total arrogance. It was all about me." He adds, "Someone once told me when your giftedness outweighs your character, implosion is always on the horizon. Well, it caught up with me and I imploded."

Justin began to understand that if there was any hope for a future with his family, he was going to have to build a foundation that was cemented in the character of Christ and allow his giftedness to flow from that. It was in his "dark night" that God began to shape my friend into the man he had imagined when he thought Justin into existence.

Justin remembers, "I lived most of my Christian life growing incrementally. I prayed and read scripture, but I still depended on myself. This situation with the affair, my separation from Trisha, and the loss of my church ushered in complete and utter brokenness. There was no hope other than the redeeming power of Christ. I could not make this up to God. I could not make this up to Trish. I was so desperate for grace and totally incapable of making myself good again. I had depended on God before when I couldn't figure stuff out, but this was different. And I'm different now. It's not that I have a low self-esteem. It's that I have a higher esteem of him. He's my only hope."

Was it different for Trisha? In her case, as for many, Plan B didn't arise from a choice or a mistake on her part—at least not on the surface. It just dropped into her lap—an unwelcome surprise.

Interestingly enough, though this Plan B situation was not Trish's fault, it still pushed her to confront her limitations, to explore the ways she might have contributed to the problem. She remembers, "My security was gone. Overnight, I became a single parent working two jobs. It was a very long process of allowing God to tear down the walls I had been building most of my adult life. Brick by brick, God would reveal layers of dysfunction he wanted to remove. It was totally appropriate for me to be ticked off. It was okay that I was devastated and wrecked. Nobody would blame me for being bitter. But I was beginning to learn that if we stay in those seasons and live out of the bitterness, it becomes dangerous. If you stay in that anger and bitterness too long it will ruin your life."

Pouring In

But there is more to the transformation of the "dark night" than God just purging our lives of sins and imperfections. He wants not only to get rid of certain things in our lives, but to pour certain things in. He's always looking for ways to infuse his love and grace into us. And that, too, requires our cooperation. It's always tempting for us to quit or even rush ahead in this transformation process. But if "we will remain still, listening for his voice, God will insert something of himself into our character that will mark the rest of our journey with him."[6]

Justin experienced that very thing when he was struggling with his humiliating Plan B. Not only was God stripping him of his arrogance and self-dependency, but he was also revealing himself in a new and fresh way. Justin remembers, "I was desperate. I had ruined my marriage. I had ruined my church. I had nobody to turn to but God. I felt totally alone. But in the moment I needed grace the most, God was there to give it to me."

I knew the Davis family well before this family crisis, but it's been amazing to watch the transformation that has happened in their lives since. With a lot of counseling, they managed to hold their marriage together. They've worked together on Justin's addiction issues, and together they have sought out new channels of ministry. But most important, the God they interacted with during their "dark night" transformed the way they do life. It transformed the way they love and serve others.

Meeting You in the Pain

Justin and Trisha's story is just one powerful example of the ways that the Plan Bs of our lives can lead to positive change. Our tragedies hold the possibility of transformation. The "dark nights" of our souls can bring the gift of true and positive change.

But this is important to recognize: it doesn't automatically happen. It is perfectly possible to live through a Plan B circumstance without learning anything, without growing closer to God, without any kind of transformation.

What makes the difference? John 15:1–5 provides a hint:

> I am the true vine; my Father is the gardener. He cuts off every branch of mine that does not produce fruit. And he trims and cleans every branch that produces fruit so that it will produce even more fruit. You are already clean because of the words I have spoken to you. Remain in me, and I will remain in you. A branch cannot produce fruit alone but must remain in the vine. In the same way, you cannot produce fruit alone but must remain in me. I am the vine, and you are the branches. If any remain in me and I remain in them, they produce much fruit. But without me they can do nothing.

The key here is remaining in him.

If true transformation is going to develop from your Plan B, there has to be this desire to "remain" or "abide" with the Lord.

And that in turn involves believing that the Lord is with us, that he understands what we're going through and knows how we feel and is there for us in our pain.

Recounting her prayer life in the days that followed the crisis, Trisha says, "At first I prayed, 'God, you have no idea what I'm going through.' But the more I prayed, the more I thought about the life of Jesus. He knows what it's been like to be betrayed by friends. He knows what's it's like to be stripped of position and humiliated. I began to realize Jesus did experience every single hurt that I had and even more. My view of Jesus changed. He can and he is a part of every single hurt that we've gone through. There is nothing so devastating that he can't redeem."

What a beautiful truth. There is no Plan B so devastating that our Lord can't redeem. There is no pain we experience that he cannot comprehend. He understands the betrayal and loss you feel. He understands the hurt and humiliation. He understands the disappointment and discouragement. He simply . . . understands. After all, he's been through it all before us. (Is there any stronger example of transformation through tragedy than the cross?) And he's there for us in the most devastating of our Plan B "dark nights."

The book of Psalms is full of brutally honest prayers from an individual whose life didn't turn out the way he had expected it to turn out. In Psalm 139 the psalmist uses three metaphors to describe three different places you would not expect to find God's presence but still do. He writes:

> *Where can I go to get away from your Spirit?*
> *Where can I run from you?*
> *If I go up to the heavens, you are there.*
> *If I lie down in the grave, you are there.*
> *If I rise with the sun in the east,*
> *and settle in the west beyond the sea,*
> *even there you would guide me,*
> *With your right hand you would hold me.*
> *I could say, "The darkness will hide me.*
> *Let the light around me turn into night."*
> *But even the darkness is not dark to you.*
> *The night is as light as the day;*
> *darkness and light are the same to you. (vv. 7–12)*

He's saying that in the most unlikely places, even there, God's presence abounds. He talks about the "heavens," the "far side of the sea," and in verse eight he mentions the "grave." This is actually the Hebrew word *sheol*.

Sheol is used throughout the Old Testament, including, but not limited to, the book of Job. Job describes it as a place that is deep (Job 11:8), dark (10:21, 22), and with bars (17:16). It's also said the dead "go down" to it (Num. 16:30, 33; Ezek. 31:15, 16, 17). This leads many to interpret *sheol* as a kind of hell.

Whether your Plan B was self-inflicted or something that has happened to you, you may well feel that it's your own little personal hell. Imagine—even there, God is fully present offering his presence to you.

That's a powerful promise for anyone living through a "dark night of the soul." It's a powerful reminder for anyone slogging through a Plan B. And it's a key to transformation in tragedy—we can abide in him because he abides with us.

Do you know what the most frequently stated promise from God in Scripture is? God promises us over and over, "I am with you." And I think there's a reason he says it so often.

I believe God knows how hard it can be to live in Plan B. (He should. In the person of Jesus Christ, he's experienced it too.) He knows how confused we get, how frustrated we get, and how lonely and isolated we may feel. So he just keeps whispering into our bruised souls this gentle reminder: *You may not sense me or feel me. But take heart because I really am here.*

Do you know what the most frequently stated promise from God in Scripture is? God promises us over and over, "I am with you."

He's inviting us to turn our cares over to him, to pour our hearts out to him, and to ask him to show himself to us. He's asking us to let him use our Plan B tragedies to transform us . . . just as Trisha and Justin Davis allowed themselves to be transformed.

Greater Than

Throughout this crisis in their marriage, the Davises learned that Jesus was larger than even this nightmare they were living. "When you're sitting in a living room telling your three young boys that Dad isn't coming home," Trisha says, "then the truth that 'Jesus is bigger' is all that you have.

"Sure, there are days I wish it would have never happened. But who our family is today and the relationships we have with each other and with God have been formed throughout this time in a way they never could have been without the pain and darkness."

If you remember the stages we talked about earlier, I would say the Davis family is now fluctuating between stages five and six. Some four years after the bomb dropped on their lives, God has begun to use them to tell their story all over the country, helping other couples caught in a web of lies. Thousands of couples are stepping out and finding help and hope because of Justin and Trisha's courageous choice to share what God taught them throughout their Plan B nightmare.

Like Justin and Trisha Davis, like St. John of the Cross, they are living out the transformative reality described by Ronald Rolheiser:

> The end result of this passage through the dark night . . . will be a fundamental change in our motivation. Instead of interacting with others and the world for the gratification, satisfaction, and pleasure they bring us, we will act out of a Christ-like desire to help others in their struggle to come into a genuine community of love, beauty, truth, and goodness, and see others in the fullness of their own uniqueness, complexity, beauty, and need for salvation.[7]

Has it ever crossed your mind that maybe, just maybe, God is using your current pain to form something beautiful inside of you? Has it ever crossed your mind that maybe this Plan B that has you struggling just might be an invitation to rest in deeper levels of his transforming presence? Is it possible God wants to use your Plan B as a megaphone to rattle your cage and keep you from settling for a mediocre, unexamined life?

I think you just might discover the change God has in mind is worth the pain of your soul's dark night. That change might be what redeems your Plan B.

That's transformation through tragedy.

FOURTEEN THE BOW

One of my primary responsibilities at the church where I pastor is teaching each weekend. This also means I get to participate in our creative team meetings, where we plan out the weekend services.

In these planning meetings we sometimes talk about what we call "the bow." It's like a bow on a package—the nice, neat conclusion we try to shoot for. The bow is that scene in the movie where suddenly the whole movie makes sense—you know, when you get your questions answered or when your tension is released.

I wish I had a nice bow for this book.

But I don't.

Have you seen those commercials for a very popular office supply store that feature what they call the "easy button"? Do you know they actually sell these? Someone bought me an easy button, and it now sits on my desk. My kids love to run into my office and press it. When you press the big red button, a booming voice says, "That was easy."

I'm afraid the church sometimes thinks there is an easy button for broken dreams, unmet expectations, and sudden crises. As Sue Monk Kidd writes, we sometimes try "to create shortcuts—promises of easy grace, push-button answers to complicated problems, illusions that we can to go church and work to bring in the kingdom out there in the world without entering the fiery process of bringing it into our own soul."[1]

And no wonder she goes on to say, "Living with questions can indeed be a miserable experience. We like things fixed, figured out, and nailed down, even if that means being nailed to a false and static existence."[2]

People who want life hammered down into tight, legalistic certainties seem to me to be the people most insecure inside. Frankly, the folks who frighten me the most are those who are dead certain about everything, who claim to have all the answers and no questions.

And here is where I think I owe those I've led, counseled, and pastored over the years an apology. I'm afraid at times I've tried to hurry people through the crisis. In my discomfort with the tension of uncertainty, I've tried to manufacture bows when they weren't appropriate. I've wanted to usher people down a path of sudden and painless spiritual transformation when in truth there is no such path.

I've discovered that sometimes God wants us to live inside of the questions. Sometimes he wants us to linger in the waiting, hoping, praying. In fact, sometimes it's right in the middle of our darkness, in the middle of our crisis, in the middle of our Plan B struggles that God speaks most clearly.

Why? Maybe it's only in that moment that we're ready to listen. I don't know for sure. But what I do know is this: questions are not bad. Quite the contrary, in fact. I've come to think we should be filled with more questions and fewer conclusions. More mystery and fewer assumptions. More wonder and fewer equations.

About a year ago, I went through a season of darkness. There was no one thing that had caused this darkness. I just felt a distance from God. To be honest, I felt alone. I was going through some very difficult leadership challenges in my church—an out-of-balance schedule, a barrage of criticism, and several personal disappointments. I had reached a personal emotional low.

I've discovered that sometimes God wants us to
live inside of the questions. Sometimes he wants
us to linger in the waiting, hoping, praying.

I was literally waiting at a red light on Hillsboro Road in front of
Green Hills Mall when God broke the silence. But let me back up to
several months earlier to give this story some context.

Earlier that year I was with Brandi and the boys in Orange
Beach, Alabama. We had been able to escape for a few days to a
great condo a generous church member had let us borrow. We had
a wonderful time just being a family and enjoying the sand, waves,
and sun.

During the vacation I misplaced my sunglasses (on average, I lose
three pair a year), so I went into this sunglasses store. There must have
been ten thousand pairs of sunglasses in this place. I tried on glasses for
at least thirty minutes and eventually emerged with a pair on. Brandi
was waiting outside, and when she saw me she said, "Pete, there were
thousands of pairs of glasses in there, and you picked those?"

I said, "What's the matter with these glasses?"

She said, "Well, for starters, they're kind of feminine."

I chalked her criticism up to not being as fashion forward as I am.

Later that night, I twittered a picture of our family that included
my new glasses. A good friend immediately sent me a text that said,
"Dude, where did you get the chick glasses?" Apparently, Brandi was
right. They were not the manliest glasses in the world.

Now, where were we?

Oh yes. Fast forward to several months later. I'm sitting at this
red light on a way home from officiating at a wedding. I'm also
contemplating on this difficult season and literally praying through
tears, asking God for help.

I took my sunglasses off to wipe my eyes. And when I did that,

I noticed an inscription on the inside of my girly glasses. It said, in very small print "Ps. 18:2."

I remember sitting there shocked. *Oh my gosh*, I thought. *These aren't just chick glasses. They're Christian chick glasses!*

I immediately grabbed the little black Bible I had just used for the wedding ceremony and looked up Psalm 18:2. I read the words out loud in the car:

> *The Lord is my rock, my protection, my Savior.*
> *My God is my rock.*
> *I can run to him for safety.*
> *He is my shield and my saving strength, my defender.*

These were the words I needed. This was the reality I was desperate to be reminded of.

Next thing I knew, I heard the sound of a honking horn. The light had turned green, and my time of waiting was over. My struggles at work didn't disappear overnight, but that sense of being alienated from God was gone.

Am I trying to say that God led some individual to start a sunglass store in Orange Beach and then led him or her to order a line of Christian-inspired sunglasses so that one day in June I would be led to pick those glasses out and in my moment of waiting and longing, God would lead me to take my glasses off and read that verse?

No, I'm not saying that God did that. But I am saying that he could have.

He could have.

I'm also saying that however it happened, it gave me what I needed.

That's the kind of God we worship. While there are not always easy solutions to our problems, God persists in finding ways to whisper into our hearts the truth that we are loved, forgiven, and constantly on his mind. I hope he has found a way to whisper in the pages of this book.

Better Than an Answer

I want you to know that my heart is heavy as I write this, probably heavier than it has been in a long time. I've spent almost a year writing this book, praying through this material, and immersing myself emotionally into the stories of dozens and dozens of individuals who have been in the midst of a Plan B. I've felt the pressure escalate as I've neared the end of the book because I so desperately want to offer you a bow. I want to tie this whole thing up nicely and neatly and lay it right before you.

And I have to be honest and say I'm weary. Hearing the stories and reading the e-mails of those who allowed me to enter their Plan Bs has been difficult. There have been times when I just sat there at my computer, reading and crying and praying for so many who are living in the pain of a difficult time in life.

I consider it a great privilege to walk with you. I'm thankful you have allowed me to accompany you to those places where you are weak, vulnerable, scared, and lonely. And at the end of this book, I have so desperately wanted to give you a bow to wrap up your experience.

But again, I don't have a bow.

I have spent a lot of time praying about how to wrap this book up. But can you put a bow on a book like this? My conclusion is no. No, you can't.

However, while I can't offer you a bow, I think I can offer you something even more profound, even more life changing, even more meaningful.

There is no bow on this book. But that's okay because Christianity doesn't always have a bow on it. There is no bow, but there is hope.

There is hope because there is the cross.

You see I've come to believe we may never be able to answer some of life's most difficult questions.

I'll never forget sitting across from a young woman in my office one day. Her face was familiar—she had started coming to our church—but I really didn't know her. I certainly didn't know her story.

She started our time together by asking me if I believed God really had formed her and knew her even in her mother's womb as Scripture stated. I quickly responded with a simple, "Yes, I do." I quoted Jeremiah 1:5:

> Before I formed you in the womb I knew you,
> before you were born I set you apart;
> I appointed you as a prophet to the nations. (NIV)

"I believe that to the core of my being," I told her.

"Okay," she said. "Do you believe God knew I was going to be born to my particular family?"

"Sure," I said.

She continued the questioning with, "Do you believe God knew I was going to fail the seventh grade?"

I smiled. "I guess so."

"Do you believe God knew I would go to the University of Alabama and graduate with a degree in elementary education?"

I said, "Yep, I do. I believe God is omniscient—meaning he knows everything before it even happens." Then I looked at her and asked, "Do you mind my asking where you're going with all of this?"

She sat there silently for a second as tears welled up in her eyes. She finally said, "What I really want to know is, if God knew all of this, why would he allow me to be born into a family where I would be sexually abused by my father for almost ten years?"

The tears ran down her face, and I realized I had no answer for her question.

Here's a portion of an e-mail I recently received from one of our church members. He wrote:

> Yesterday morning, my cousin's four-year-old son died from a brain tumor. He was diagnosed just fifty-five days ago, went into a coma ten days ago, and passed away yesterday. The family was on their last day of a Make-A-Wish Foundation trip to Disney World when Josiah slipped into a coma. This family's life has been turned upside down in less than two months. The most obvious question is: What is God's purpose in allowing a little child like that to die from such a detestable disease?

Once again, I realized I didn't have a good answer.

Oh, I could dig in my books and come up with answers that have been given for the "problem of suffering." I could dig up my theodicy notes from seminary and give some ideas. (Theodicy is a branch of philosophy and theology that attempts to justify the ways of God in the presence of evil.) I could trot out a lot of what I've said in this book about how God is with us and how he transforms us in tragedy.

But I still didn't have any answers that would fully satisfy in a circumstance like this. No answers that would bring complete closure or comfort.

So when it comes to Plan Bs, I'm left with saying, "I don't know."

Why did you lose the baby? I don't know.

Why did he leave you? I don't know.

Why did the bottom drop out for you financially? I don't know.

As long as you live on this earth you may walk around with some huge unanswered questions. I suspect I will too. God simply doesn't answer many of these questions for us. What we come up with are basically just guesses, attempts to get our minds around the unanswerable, and efforts to reach out and help each other.

If you are a Christian, you may already know all this. If you are a Christian, you're accustomed to holding two seemingly contradictory realities together in your mind and heart. (Some days you may hold them together more easily than others.)

One reality is God's love and care for us in every aspect of our lives, which we know from Scripture and from our own personal experience is real. You can probably recount time after time when God showed his love to you through his faithfulness and kindness. I know I can.

But the second reality you must balance is disappointment, heartbreak, and pain. You've experienced this in your own life, and you've seen it in the lives of friends and in the form of national and global disasters.

It seems hardly a day goes by that we don't witness a collision between these two realities. How can we reconcile these two unmixable components: a God of love who is all-powerful and the universal experience of tragedy and suffering?

This, my friends, is an enormous puzzle, and I can't solve it for you. I can't solve it for myself either. I can't fully answer this question because I don't believe God fully answers that question. He gives lots of evidence, but no definitive answers. I'm not sure our finite minds could comprehend the real answer to that question.

But let me repeat: Instead of an answer, God offers us something better. He offers us a solution. He offers us the cross.

Ever since the Fall, you see, we've had this problem with sin and evil. This world is broken and stained with sin and not the way it's supposed to be. Bad things happen to good people. Good people do bad things. Lots of people suffer in ways far out of proportion to what they have done. In a way, the Fall was the original Plan B, the source of all our frustrating, heartbreaking Plan B situations.

But immediately after the Fall, God went to work on a plan to bring redemption to each of us. He gathered a people and taught them about himself. He showed them his faithfulness and mercy, punished and forgave them, taught them who he was and how to live together. And then, when the time was right, he sent his Son, Jesus, who conquered the sin and death that originated through the Fall.

Instead of an answer, God offers us something better.
He offers us a solution. He offers us the cross.

Because of Jesus, suffering is never the last word. We're promised if we will put our trust in him, there will be a day when he "will wipe away every tear from [our] eyes, and there will be no more death, sadness, crying, or pain, because all the old ways are gone" (Rev. 21:4).

That's the promise. That's the last word—that ultimately God will defeat the pain and heartbreak of this world. That he's already defeated it, but we're just living out the aftermath of the battle. That there will be a day when all is restored.

But here is where faith comes into play. Here's where choice comes in the middle of a situation you probably didn't choose.

If you're in the midst of a Plan B situation or if you're still reeling from one, then you're continuing to flatten your nose against those two contradictory realities: a loving God and a broken life full of pain.

And every time you confront it, you're left with a choice. The choice of faith.

Faith is saying I choose to believe in you, God, more than this or that tragedy. I throw myself in utter dependence on you—you alone, a God who specializes in resurrections, a God who brings hope to the hopeless, a God who is a father to the fatherless, a God who was willing to send your Son to a cross to prove that you are more powerful than the worst thing evil could do.

Scripture reminds us again and again that this suffering we experience is only temporary. Scripture insists there will be a day when God brings resolution and redemption to your Plan B suffering:

> *Crying may last for a night,*
> *but joy comes in the morning (Ps. 30:5)*

The sufferings we have now are nothing compared to the great glory that will be shown to us (Rom. 8:18).

Some of this resolution may well happen in this life. Your current Plan B may well turn out for the best. Things may get better, even if they don't turn out the way you planned. In fact, things probably will get better.

You might be able to reconcile with your spouse, or you may be able to build a satisfying life without your spouse.

You might get well, or you might learn to manage your illness.

You might get your job back, or you might find an entirely new career.

It's also possible that things will get worse, not better. You might face one Plan B after another, maybe the rest of your life. And even if things get better, you might have to live all your life with the pain of what you had and lost. All your life, part of you will probably mourn the death of your original dream.

Even then, we still have the promise that eventually, somehow, some way, all will be made right. And in the meantime, in the midst of our suffering, we have God's presence, which we experience through faith. We have hope, which comes through faith. We have growth and possibilities, which begin with the choice of faith.

Because we're back to the choice. It always comes back to the choice of faith. It's the fundamental choice that changes everything in our Plan Bs because it changes who we become.

Choose to Let God Change You

One of my favorite pastimes as a child was playing with modeling clay. I never had a real talent for molding and shaping things, but I've always really enjoyed it. Truth be told, I still like playing with the stuff—even though it played a role in one of my most embarrassing moments as a parent.

Cross Point was only a few years old, and I went to pick up my then four-year-old son, Jett, from his class. Their lesson on that particular day was on Noah's ark. His teacher's name was Lori. Lori was your stereotypical super-sweet Sunday school teacher who was a bit on the conservative side. She had a few children of her own who were truly angels—the best-behaved kids I've ever met.

For her lesson on Noah's ark, Lori handed out blobs of the dough and told each kid to shape his or her blob into one of the animals that Noah took on the ark with him.

She then proceeded to go around the room and had all the children tell the class what animal they had made. She said when she got to Jett, she very confidently asked him if he had made a snake. He said, "No, Miss Lori. This is actually a penis." (Of all the teachers it had to be Miss Lori. Of all the kids it had to be mine.)

Don't worry. There is actually a point to this little story. Because the Old Testament repeatedly (Isaiah 29:16; 45:9; 64:8) compares God to a Potter and us to the clay. And Jeremiah 18:3–4 says:

> So I went down to the potter's house and saw him working at the potter's wheel. He was using his hands to make a pot from clay, but something went wrong with it. So he used that clay to make another pot the way he wanted it to be. Then the LORD spoke his word to me: "Family of Israel, can't I do the same thing with you?" says the LORD. "You are in my hands like the clay in the potter's hands."

The idea is that God has the ability to form and shape us into the people we need to be. He has made us, and he can remake us as well.

God can take the pain and hurt you've experienced and use it to expand and mold your heart to reflect his heart.

The question is, do you think you can sacrifice who you are today for who you could become?

That's one choice of faith—to let God change you. To give him permission and leeway to make you into the person he has in mind.

Mark Batterson explains the same choice a different way:

> If you feel like you're stuck in a tragedy, here's my advice: give Jesus complete editorial control over your life. You have to quit trying to write your own story. And you need to accept Jesus not only as Lord and Savior but also as Author. If you allow Him to begin writing His-story through your life, it'll give the tragedy a fairy-tale ending. I'm not promising a life without heartache or pain or loss but I am promising a different ending.[3]

The Choice to Love

Not long ago I spent ten days in India with Compassion International trying to bring attention to their child sponsorship programs. While there, I saw some of the worst human suffering I've ever seen. The "why" question plagued me the entire time we were there. I watched over and over collision between the two contradicting realities of God's love and a broken world.

On one particular day we went to a place called "the home for the dying." This is a ministry Mother Teresa of Calcutta set up to minister to people in their final days of life. It was packed beyond capacity with people struggling for their lives. In fact, it was so full that to get into the place we had to walk around or step over the bodies of people who were waiting on the steps to get in.

I walked from cot to cot to cot holding hands, whispering prayers, and looking into the eyes of men and women who were in their final days of life. Most had been plagued by devastating diseases that had consigned them to lives of pain and misery for years with little or no pain medication.

I remember walking away from that place and feeling a heavy weight on my chest. Experiencing that much suffering and death in that small amount of time will do that to you.

I wondered, *How did Mother Teresa do this every day? How could she immerse herself into this much suffering day in and day out?*

Interestingly enough, she answered me, posthumously, through something I read. It's one of my favorite Mother Teresa quotes: "For when you suffer this way, mysteriously, more space opens up for you to receive the love of Jesus."[4]

Somehow, mysteriously, when we receive the love of Jesus into our lives through suffering, when we decide to *choose* that love and share it, we keep suffering from having the last word in our lives.

I think the key word there is *mysteriously*. Somehow, when we go through a Plan B, the experience provides an opportunity for us to choose to receive the love of Jesus in a unique way. Somehow, mysteriously, when we receive the love of Jesus into our lives through suffering, when we decide to *choose* that love and share it, we keep suffering from having the last word in our lives.

Choosing love, in fact, somehow empowers us to reflect God to others in the world more clearly and consistently than we ever have. In denying our self-centered tendencies, we're able to serve and be served, forgive and be forgiven, care and be cared for. Our joy is no longer fueled by getting what we want, but by having God live in us and through us.

The choice for love, like the choice of faith, can be painful. But as Henri Nouwen writes, as we continue to make the sometimes painful choice of love, we grow:

> The pain that comes from deep love makes your love ever more fruitful. It is like a plow that breaks the ground to allow the seed to take root and grow into a strong plant. Every time you experience the pain of rejection, absence, or death, you are faced with a choice. You can become bitter and decide not to love again, or you can stand straight in your pain and let the soil on which you stand become richer and more able to give life to new seeds.
>
> The more you have loved and have allowed yourself to suffer because of your love, the more you will be able to let your heart grow wider and deeper.[5]

The Choice to Trust

That brings us to the end of this book, and I have no cute bows or surprise endings to wrap up your messy Plan B circumstances. I have no easy button for you to push.

What I do have to offer you is a cross. A cross that communicates how much God loves you and how far he'll go to begin the reconciliation of the entire created order (including your Plan B pain) through the shedding of his Son's blood.

I believe the message of that cross. I believe there is a God who has chosen to take the full weight of human suffering and cosmic evil upon himself. I believe there is a God who says through that cross, I love you. I am in control. And I can use your worst experiences for eternal good.

The cross is proof that he does not always change the circumstance, but that he works every circumstance to his purpose. He will never let go of us. His cross will be an anchor of hope for us.

Do you still have questions? So do I.

Do you wonder how long the Plan B situation will last? I don't know.

Why is this happening? I don't know.

Will it end soon? I don't know.

Will we ever understand our Plan B dilemmas?

On this side of heaven, quite possibly not.

Does the way we respond to them matter?

More than you will ever know.

I once heard pastor Matt Chandler say in a message that there is a big difference between trust and understanding. Trust is what we need when we don't have understanding.[6]

The apostle Paul wrote in Romans 15:13, "I pray that the God who gives hope will fill you with much joy and peace while you trust in him. Then your hope will overflow by the power of the Holy Spirit."

Will we ever understand our Plan B dilemmas?
On this side of heaven, quite possibly not.
Does the way we respond to them matter?
More than you will ever know.

Notice the promise here. The God of hope will fill your life with joy and peace and you will overflow with hope. Wow! And isn't that exactly what you need right now in the midst of your Plan B?

But there's a condition—that you trust him. Trust is the choice that gets you through Plan B.

So I'm not tying this book up with a bow. I'm not asking you to understand. But I am asking you to trust the God who loves you.

The God who has promised to be with you. The God who right now is engaged in the mysterious process of reshaping you into who you need to be. The God who can bring you joy and peace and hope.

I'm asking you to trust that one day faith will win over doubt, that light will win over darkness, that love will win over hate, and that all things will one day be redeemed. I'm asking you, right in the middle of your Plan B pain, to trust the process that is going on in your life.

It won't be finished for a while, but it has begun.

God will finish what he started.

Wait for it.

FOR THOUGHT
AND DISCUSSION

Chapter 1: Reality

1. Has there ever been a season in your life when you looked at your circumstances and wondered if God really cared?
2. Give an example of a time when you realized some area of your life wasn't going to turn out the way you had hoped.
3. Do you ever get frustrated looking at other people's lives and thinking that life seems to be working for them and not you? How do you handle that frustration?
4. Which is a bigger problem for you—believing in God or dealing with the reality that God does exist yet so does a lot of pain and suffering?
5. What is your typical response when God doesn't show up for you the way you thought God was going to show up?

Chapter 2: Don't Run

1. Do you remember a time when all the circumstances of your life led you to believe a certain dream was going to become reality . . . only to have that dream shatter (or fizzle)?

2. Do you see any similarities between your life and the first half of David's story?

3. When you feel as if God is not there and life is not turning out the way you had planned, how do you typically respond?

  • I tend to lean into God more than ever before.

  • I tend to try to take control by manipulating the circumstances so they'll come out as I think they should.

  • I try to minimize the circumstances and pretend it's not a big deal.

  • I'm often tempted to turn toward addictive behavior (overeating, alcohol, television, work) to minimize the pain.

  • I do something else, for example:

  _____

4. James 1:12 says, "Blessed is the man who perseveres under trial, because when he has stood the test, he will receive the crown of life that God has promised to those who love him" (NIV). Can you think of a time when perseverance and patience have paid off for you in the midst of a Plan B? Can you name a time when you think your perseverance and patience did not pay off? Why do you think this is true?

Chapter 3: The Illusion of Control

1. What do you think about the following statement: "The greatest of all illusions is the illusion of control"?

2. In what area of your life are you most tempted to try to control things (vocational, relational, and/or spiritual)? What are some of the ways you try to do this?

3. David comes to a place in his life where he understands that just because his will won't be done, that doesn't mean God's will won't be done. Have you come to the same conclusion in

your life, or do your dreams, your desires, or your will still trump God's dreams, desires, and will?

4. Is complete and utter abandonment even a desire of your heart? What single step could you take in your life to assure moving in this direction?

5. Can you think of a time when you responded to a disappointment or a shattered dream in one of the following ways?
   - With ongoing anger and bitterness.
   - By trying harder to control the situation.
   - By letting go and saying, "Not my will, but your will be done."

   Why do you think you responded that way?

6. In what area of your life do you find it hardest to say "I can't" or "let it be"? Why do you think control is such an issue for you in that area?

7. Can giving up control ever be a form of irresponsibility? What determines the difference between a healthy "let it be" and an unhealthy refusal to take responsibility?

Chapter 4: Your Jordan

1. How have you seen different Plan B situations in your life stretch you and draw you closer to God? Have you ever had a Plan B situation that *didn't* do that? Why do you think that was?

2. Can you think of a time when God led you to do something you simply could not do apart from God—a time when it seemed like things moved from difficult to almost impossible? What did you do?

3. Name a time in your life when you were sure you were at a dead end with no answers . . . yet you were probably exactly where God wanted you to be?

4. "Everybody faces a Jordan. Every one of us faces a barrier that is keeping us from the life God has for us." Is there a place in your life where you sense God is asking you to take a step of faith (finances, an addiction, a relationship that's falling apart, forgiveness)?

5. Why do you think God often waits for us to take the first step before we see his power released in our lives?

6. Do you agree with the following statement: "Constant contact with the Creator is essential for transformation living"? What are some of the most effective ways to maintain contact with God?

Chapter 5: Paralyzed

1. What are you most afraid of in life? What kinds of fear tend to paralyze you?

2. What is your most common response to fear?
   - I run in the opposite direction.
   - I look fear in the eye and run right toward it.
   - I typically see fear as an opportunity to lean on God and to grow closer to him.

3. In what ways have you seen your fears establish the limits of your life?

4. Do you agree that we have all been inwardly fashioned for faith, not for fear and worry? What are some of the ways that fear, worry, and stress can harm us?

5. Oswald Chambers said, "The remarkable thing about fearing God is that when you fear God you fear nothing else, whereas if you do not fear God you fear everything else." In what ways have you seen that play out in your life?

6. What is one fear you feel you need to surrender to God or one area of your life where you need to seek God's kingdom first?

Chapter 6: Whiplash

1. Have you ever walked into a situation thinking it was going to work out great, only to feel as if the rug had been ripped out from underneath you? Describe this situation.

2. When is the last time you asked (or wanted to ask), "Why me?"—or just "Why?"

3. Why do you think it's so hard for us to imagine God is with us when we're in the midst of a Plan B situation?

4. When was the last time you felt like Paul, stuck in Troas, not knowing what God wanted you to do next? How did you handle it?

5. What do you think someone who is in your exact circumstances would do if they were confident God was with them?

6. Rick Warren says, "God is more interested in your character than your comfort." What about you? Are you more committed to your comfort or character? Are you sure?

7. Are you ever tempted to put your faith in what God does instead of who God is?

Chapter 7: What Have You Done for Me Lately?

1. In what ways/circumstances are you sometimes tempted to view God as a vending machine? Has this ever seemed to work for you?

2. Describe a time when you fell into temptation because your needs weren't being met. What happened in this situation? How do you think you could have handled it differently?

3. Can you remember a time when you felt you were doing everything right but you were still "punished"? Can you remember a time when you really messed up but somehow got away with it? How did you react in either situation?

4. Have you ever felt completely abandoned by God? If so, how did this happen? If not, what circumstances would tend to make you feel that way?

5. What are some of the circumstances you are most grateful for in life? What are some circumstances that *don't* naturally evoke feelings of gratitude? How do you respond to the idea of receiving *all* of your life—even the hard stuff—as a gift? What would keep you from being able to do that?

6. Do you find it difficult to just "believe God is who he says he is"? Why do you think this is so hard for some people to do?

Chapter 8: Darkness

1. Have you always assumed, like so many others, that the Bible promises God will never give us more than we can handle? Why do you think the chapter calls this "whacked theology"?

2. Has God ever asked you to give up something you were clinging to, something that might have kept you from deeper intimacy with him? How did you respond?

3. Do you have a systematic way for remembering God's faithfulness in your life? If not, what are some ways you can establish one?

4. Do you agree with the following statement: "God loves you enough to strip you of the things that keep you from him"? What are some specific "good things" in life that might keep a person from God? Have you ever known a situation like this—where good things actually hindered a person's walk with God?

5. This chapter suggests that doubting can actually be an act of faith. Do you agree? Why or why not?

Chapter 9: Me Too

1. Can you think of a time when someone comforted you with the words "me too" (or similar words)? How about a time when you were able to comfort someone with those same words?
2. What constitutes the "winners' circle" in your life? What is the "losers' circle"? Do you agree that it is usually easier to find authentic community in a losers' circle? Why or why not?
3. How do you feel about the following statement: "You can only be loved to the extent you are known"?
4. Have you seen how prideful, arrogant, judgmental attitudes have been destructive to community and ultimately your own spiritual growth? Describe how this happened.
5. Why do you think more people don't feel comfortable to share their disappointments, hurts, and questions in the context of Christian community?
6. What are some specific ways you can follow Paul's command in Galatians 6:2 to "help each other with . . . troubles"?

Chapter 10: The Anchor

1. Describe a time when you've felt you were at odds with God. Do you think it was because you didn't really want God but wanted what you thought God could give you? Do you think this chapter makes an unfair accusation in this regard?
2. This chapter speaks of two jacked-up theologies, two inadequate mental frameworks that can result from an incomplete reading of John 16:33. What are these? Can you think of anyone you know who subscribes to each of these incomplete approaches? Which do you personally think is more dangerous or harmful?

3. What common mistake about Christianity does this chapter point out? How would this mistake affect the way we approach a Plan B situation?

4. What are some idols you have noticed the people in your life worshiping? What idols might be revealed if you were to follow the trail of your time, your affections, your energy, and your money?

5. What do you think about the statement, "We must be willing, if necessary, to abandon the life we've planned and dreamed of in order to receive the life that our God has authored for us"? Do you know anyone who has actually done that?

Chapter 11: Power and Hope

1. Have you ever thought about the emotions that were represented at the cross? As a follower of Christ, what emotions do you think you would have felt that day?

2. How do you typically respond to situations that feel out of control or that make you feel powerless? For instance, are you likely to work harder, to try to get things organized, to try to get away from the situation, or to lean more on God?

3. If you could have any superpower, what would it be? What do you think this says about your needs, your hopes, and your fears?

4. This chapter suggests that our desire for power is really a desire for hope. Do you agree with this? Why or why not?

5. According to this chapter, what are the two kinds of hope? Which kind of hope is more dependable, and why?

6. What does it really mean to say that the same power that raised Christ from the dead is still available to us today? How would our lives change if we really believed that?

7. In what area of your life do you most need a miracle right now?

Chapter 12: Waiting on God

1. St Augustine said, "There are two things that kill the soul: despair and false hope." Can you think of a time you had false hope?

2. Has there ever been a time you've felt God calling you to give him glory in a way you just weren't excited about?

3. Do you tend to be a *quickaholic*? How have you seen that play out in your spiritual formation?

4. The Bible is full of example after example of people waiting on God. What do you think God is trying to teach you in the waiting these days?

5. Does it bother you that Jesus waited so long before going to be with Mary and Martha?

6. How do you feel about having to accept God's timing along with his power?

7. Lewis Smedes said, "Waiting is our destiny." How do you tend to respond to waiting? Do you consider yourself a patient person or an impatient person?

8. Psalm 62:5–6 says, "Find rest, O my soul, in God alone; my hope comes from him. He alone is my rock and my salvation; he is my fortress, I will not be shaken." What kind of comfort do you find in a verse like this?

Chapter 13: Transformation Through Tragedy

1. On a scale of 1–10, how busy do you think you are these days? Is there room in your schedule to live an "examined" life? In general, do you feel fulfilled in your life?

2. How do you respond to the idea that we may *need* our Plan Bs to rescue us from a busy or shallow life? Do you find that statement enlightening, insulting, confusing? Do you agree?

3. Peter Scazzero says, "Our culture routinely interprets losses as alien invasions that interrupt our 'normal' lives. We numb our pain through denial, blaming, rationalizations, addictions, and avoidance." When you experience pain, how are you most likely to numb it?

4. At what stage of spiritual development (as described in this chapter) would you say you're in right now? Do you think it's possible to go back and repeat a stage?

5. What does this chapter say is the key to being transformed in a Plan B situation?

6. What do you think God might be saying to you in the midst of your Plan B right now? (If you're not currently in a Plan B situation, try to recall some of the things you learned about God and yourself in a previous Plan B situation.)

Chapter 14: The Bow

1. On a scale of 1–10, how important is it to you to have things fixed, figured out, and nailed down? What do you tend to do when you can't tie a bow on things?

2. Name some times when God showed his love and faithfulness toward you. Then name a time when you were painfully aware of the tragedy and suffering? How do you tend to reconcile the seemingly contradictory realities of a God of love who is all-powerful and a life filled with tragedy and suffering?

3. Can you think of an example from your life where you chose to believe in God more than the crisis or tragedy in your life? What was the outcome of that situation?

4. What are the choices we always have in a Plan B circumstance? What choices might we not have?

5. Somehow, mysteriously, when we receive the love of Jesus into our lives through suffering, when we decide to *choose* that

love and share it, we keep suffering from having the last word in our lives. What are some of the specific ways we can *choose* and *share* the love of Jesus in the midst of our suffering?

6. Have you ever had a moment in the midst of a crisis when God unmistakably communicated to you that he was still with you? How did this come about?

7. What does the cross of Jesus Christ communicate to you in the midst of your Plan B?

NOTES

Chapter 1: Reality

1. This little passage is widely quoted, but there's quite a bit of disagreement about the original source. Some attribute it to the novelist W. Somerset Maughan. Others credit the more contemporary Douglas Noel Adams or a man named Robert Anthony. I haven't been able to pin it down with certainty, but I think it's powerful. If you know the true author, please let me know, and I'll give full credit!

Chapter 2: Don't Run

1. I first heard this idea in a sermon by Andy Stanley, pastor of North Point Community Church in Alpharetta, Georgia. His thoughts about David can be heard firsthand in the four-part audio series, *Lessons from the Life of David*, CD-ROM (Alpharetta, GA: North Point Resources), available at http://resources.northpoint.org/store/shop.do?cID=10&pID=217.
2. John Quincy Adams, quoted in Martin Kelly, "Quotes from John Quincy Adams," About.com: American History, www.americanhistory.about.com/cs/johnquincyadams/a/quotejqadams.htm.
3. Peter Scazzero, *Emotionally Healthy Spirituality: Unleash the Power of Life in Christ* (Nashville: Thomas Nelson, 2006), 139.
4. Charles R. Swindoll, *David: A Man of Passion and Destiny*, vol. 1, Great Lives from God's Word (Nashville: Thomas Nelson, 1997), 66.
5. C. S. Lewis, *The Screwtape Letters: With Screwtape Proposes a Toast* (New York: Harper Collins, 2001), 167.

Chapter 3: The Illusion of Control

1. Scazzero, *Emotionally Healthy Spirituality*, 129.

Chapter 4: Your Jordan

1. *Strong's Hebrew Dictionary*, s. v. *Yarden* (Strong's #3383), www
.strongsnumbers.com/hebrew/3383.htm (accessed 23 Oct 2009).

Chapter 5: Paralyzed

1. Erwin McManus, "Fear" (MP3 audio file), from the teaching series *Falling Forward* (Awaken Resources, 28 Sept 2008), www.pluggd.tv/audio/channels/mosaic/episodes/4lfh5 (accessed 23 Oct 2009).
2. Earl Nightingale, "The Fog of Worry (Only 8% of Worries Are Worth It)," from *The Essence of Success*, ed. Carson V. Conant, quoted on Nightingale-Conant Web site, www.nightingale.com/AE_Article~i~210~article~TheFog ofWorryOnly8WorthIt.aspx.
3. Warren W. Wiersbe, *The Bible Exposition Commentary* (Wheaton, IL: Victor, 1996), s. v. Matthew 6:19.
4. Oswald Chambers, *The Pilgrim's Song Book* (London: Simpkin Marshall, 1949), 24. Digital ed. posted 7 Aug 2006 by Holiness Data Ministry, http://wesley .nnu.edu/wesleyctr/books/2501-2600/HDM2588.PDF.

Chapter 6: Whiplash

1. The ideas in this passage are based on Andy Stanley, *The Legend of Joe Jacobson*, DVD-ROM (Alpharetta, GA: North Point Resources), available from http://resources.northpoint.org/store/shop.do?cID=10&pID=217.
2. Tammy Trent told me her story in a personal interview, dated 5 Aug 2009. For telling her story, I've also drawn on the following: Mike Rimmer, "Tammy Trent: Living Through Personal Tragedy and Finding Healing;" CrossRythms: Christian Radio Online, www.crossrhythms.co.uk/articles/music/Tammy_ Trent_Living_Through_Personal_Tragedy_And_Finding_Gods_ Healing/26866/p1; Scott Ross, "Tammy Trent: Love Story Lost," CBN Music, www.cbn.com/cbnmusic/interviews/700club_tammytrent1101.aspx; and Tammy Trent, *Learning to Breathe Again: Choosing Life and Finding Hope* (Nashville: Thomas Nelson, 2006).
3. Rick Warren in a 28 March 2005, interview with Paul Bradshaw, quoted in Youth with a Mission North American Office, "Rick Warren on the Purpose of Life," posted 29 Jan 2009, www.usrenewal.org/?p=1594 (accessed 23 Oct 2009).

4. Erwin McManus, "God's Will" (MP3 audio file), from the teaching series *Practical Wisdom* (Awaken Resources, published 27 July 2008), www.podpoint .net/Mosaic/God_s_Will (accessed 23 Oct 2009).

5. C. S. Lewis, *The Complete C. S. Lewis* (New York: HarperCollins Signature Classics, 2002), 338.

Chapter 7: What Have You Done for Me Lately?

1. This analogy suggested by Ronald Rolheiser, *The Shattered Lantern: Recovering a Felt Presence of God* (New York: Crossroad, 2005), 80.

2. A. W. Tozer, *The Pursuit of God* (Project Gutenberg, 2008), chap. 2, www .gutenberg.org/files/25141/25141-h/25141-h.htm.

3. Scazzero, *Emotionally Healthy Spirituality*, 122–23.

4. Rolheiser, *The Shattered Lantern*, 163.

5. Andy Stanley, "Right Where You Want 'Em," part three of *The Legend of Joe Jacobson*.

Chapter 8: Darkness

1. Janet O. Hagberg and Robert A. Guelich, *The Critical Journey: Stages in the Life of Faith*, 2nd ed. (Salem, WI: Sheffield, 2004), 114–15.

2. Jeff Henderson, "Forgotten" (MP3 audio file), from the teaching series *The Waiting Room*, preached 12 July 2009 at Buckhead Community Church, Atlanta, Georgia, www.buckheadchurch.org/messages (accessed 24 Oct 2009).

3. Hagberg and Guelich, *The Critical Journey*, 114–15.

4. John Ortberg, "When God Seems Absent," on Christianity.com Web site, http://www.christianity.com/11550260/.

5. *Strong's Hebrew Dictionary*, s.v. *shalom* (Strong's #7965), www.strongsnumbers .com/hebrew/7965.htm; David Silver, "The Meaning of the Word 'Shalom,'" The Refiner's Fire: Revealing Biblical Truth in a World of Myth and Fiction, www.therefinersfire.org/meaning_of_shalom.htm; Jacques B. Doukhan, "Shalom: The Hebrew View of Peace," Shabbat Shalom: The Journal of Jewish-Christian Reconciliation, vol. 41, no. 1, 1994, www.shabbatshalom .info/article.php?id=106.

6. Jacques Ellul, *Hope in Time of Abandonment* (Harrisburg, PA: Seabury, 1973), 205.

7. Scazzero, *Emotionally Healthy Spirituality*, 146.

Chapter 9: Me Too

1. Anne Lamott, quoted in Rob Bell, *Jesus Wants to Save Christians: A Manifesto for the Church in Exile* (Grand Rapids, MI: Zondervan, 2008), 151.

2. Dallas Willard, *Hearing God: Developing a Conversational Relationship with God* (Downers Grove, IL: InterVarsity, 1984), 24.

3. Thomas Merton, *Thoughts in Solitude* (New York: Farrar, Straus and Giroux, 1958), 3.

4. Thomas Merton, *New Seeds of Contemplation* (New York: New Directions, 1972), 35.

5. *Alcoholics Anonymous: The Story of How Many Thousands of Men and Women Have Recovered from Alcoholism*, 4th ed. (New York: Alcoholics Anonymous World Services, 2001), 59.

6. Ibid.

7. Philip Yancey, *Reaching for the Invisible God: What Can We Expect to Find?* (Grand Rapids, MI: Zondervan, 2000), 170.

Chapter 10: The Anchor

1. Jurgen Moltmann, *The Crucified God: The Cross of Christ as the Foundation and Criticism of Christian Theology* (Minneapolis, MN: Fortress, 1993), 36.

2. Louie Giglio is an innovative pastor, communicator, and worship leader—the founder of Choice Ministries and the powerful Passion conferences. He is currently in the process of establishing Passion City Church in Atlanta, Georgia. The insights attributed to him in this chapter come from notes I took during a church service several years ago in Atlanta, Georgia, as Giglio spoke on the topic of dealing with difficult times as a believer, one of his messages in the four-part series "Soundtrack."

3. Ibid.

Chapter 12: Waiting on God

1. Lewis Smedes, *Standing on the Promises: Keeping Hope Alive for a Tomorrow We Cannot Control* (Nashville: Thomas Nelson, 1998), 53.

2. Francis Chan, "More Than a Follower," *Relevant*, 21 August 2008, http:// www.relevantmagazine.com/god/deeper-walk/features/1472-more-than-a-follower.

3. Smedes, *Standing on the Promises*, 41.

4. Henri Nouwen, "A Spirituality of Waiting," *Weavings* 1 (Jan-Feb 1987), 14, quoted in Sue Monk Kidd, *When the Heart Waits: Spiritual Direction for Life's Sacred Questions* (New York: HarperOne, 2006), 112.

5. Ibid.

6. Mark Batterson, *Wild Goose Chase: Reclaim the Adventure of Pursuing God* (Sisters, OR.: Multnomah, 2008), 137.

7. Kidd, *When the Heart Waits*, 19.

8. Kidd, *When the Heart Waits*, 37.

Chapter 13: Transformation Through Tragedy

1. Henri J. M. Nouwen, *Making All Things New: An Introduction to the Spiritual Life* (New York: Harper & Row, 1981), 23–4.

2. C. S. Lewis, *The Problem of Pain* (New York: HarperCollins, 2001), 91.

3. Scazzero, *Emotionally Healthy Spirituality*, 135–36.

4. Hagberg and Guelich, *The Critical Journey*.

5. Rolheiser, *The Shattered Lantern*, 87.

6. Scazzero, *Emotionally Healthy Spirituality*, 124.

7. Rolheiser, *The Shattered Lantern*, 84.

Chapter 14: The Bow

1. Kidd, *When the Heart Waits*, 25.

2. Ibid.

3. Batterson, *Wild Goose Chase*, 125.

4. Mother Teresa, source unknown.

5. Henri J. M. Nouwen, *The Inner Voice of Love: A Journey Through Anguish to Freedom* (New York: Doubleday/Image, 1999), 59.

6. Matt Chandler is the lead pastor/teaching pastor of the Village Church in Dallas, Texas. This quote is from notes I took during one of his sermons, April 2008.

ABOUT THE AUTHOR

Lee Steffen, http://leesteffen.com

Pete Wilson is the founding and senior pastor of Cross Point Church in Nashville, Tennessee, the second church he has planted in the last seven years. Pete graduated from Western Kentucky University with a degree in communications and then attended seminary at Southern Seminary in Louisville, Kentucky.

Pete's desire is to see churches become radically devoted to Christ, irrevocably committed to one another, and relentlessly dedicated to reaching those outside of God's family. He is married to Brandi Wilson, and they have three wild boys: Jett, Gage, and Brewer.

For more information about Pete's ministry, family, and leadership, visit withoutwax.tv where he blogs regularly.

VISIT PLANBBOOK.COM TO EXPERIENCE THE FULL PLAN B COMMUNITY.

- Teaching videos
- Plan B community— Share your story and read others'!
- Free teaching resources for churches
- Additional study materials

CPSIA information can be obtained at www.ICGtesting.com
Printed in the USA
LVOW06s0828031014

407073LV00006B/22/P